LYLE ASHTON HARRIS

The Tate Photography Series is a celebration of international and British photography in the Tate collection and an introduction to some of the most significant photographers at work today. Previous sets of four in the series have explored the themes of Community and Solidarity, and Ecology and Environment.

Each book focuses on an individual photographer and features a specially selected sequence of photographs, an introduction by a Tate curator and a conversation with, or statement by, the artist. These collaborative books as dialogues between artists and experts aim to enrich our understanding of photography and its connection to everyday life, and collectively they move from city streets to seashores, across landscapes and subcultures, through identities and interiors, in a visual travelogue of our world today.

The theme for Series Three is Queer and Visible, bringing together four artists who use photography to unfold valuable insights into queer life. Each artist uniquely reflects upon societal constructs of sexuality and race, and responds to the experience of living in a predominantly white and heteronormative society.

To see and to make seen, to work in good faith, to produce artful storytelling and resonant images – these are the qualities we seek from good photography. The artist-photographer notices and captures, calls for a moment of our divided and hurried attention, and reveals connection and pattern, emotion and meaning. The work sets out to expand the possible and make hearts and minds more spacious.

Series Three

3:1 **LAURA AGUILAR**
3:2 **SUNIL GUPTA**
3:3 **LYLE ASHTON HARRIS**
3:4 **AJAMU X**

LYLE ASHTON HARRIS

Edited by
Fiontán Moran

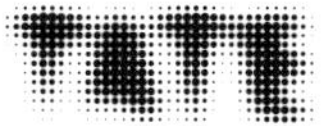

First published 2025 by order of the Tate Trustees
by Tate Publishing, a division of Tate Enterprises Ltd,
Millbank, London SW1P 4RG
www.tate.org.uk/publishing

A catalogue record for this book is available from the British Library

ISBN 978 1 84976 954 9

Distributed in the United States and Canada
by ABRAMS, New York

Library of Congress Control Number applied for

Series Editor: Simon Armstrong
Senior Editor: Nicola Bion
Production: Bill Jones
Picture Research: Roz Hill
Designed by Sarah Boris
Colour reproduction by Westerham Press, London
Printed and bound in the UK by Westerham Press, London

Front cover: *The Child* 1994
Back cover top: *Construct #10* 1989
Back cover bottom: Untitled (*Missy Elliot #35*) 2000

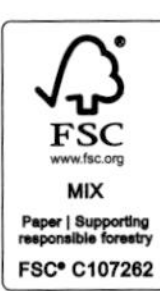

CONTENTS

INTRODUCTION

Using only two wigs, a piece of fabric, and a black seamless paper backdrop, Lyle Ashton Harris created *Constructs #10 – #13* 1989, an exploration of photography's relationship to identity and performance. Across four black-and-white photographs, Harris used his body to channel a range of references including Robert Mapplethorpe's images of Black men, fashion and ballet poses, queer culture, and classical sculpture. Through these explorations the work both declares a position and poses questions at the intersection of race and sexuality. It shows the act of self-representation, the embodiment of the self itself, as a form of drag, and how the notion of identity as in flux, how it is – as the title suggests – a construct. Created in the midst of the AIDS epidemic and the continual prejudice against gay and trans people, *Constructs #10 – #13* was a political declaration too – an assertion of an identity that does not seek to explain but simply is. First publicly exhibited in 1990 at Camerawork in London, *Constructs #10 – #13* came to prominence in 1994 when it was included in Thelma Golden's landmark exhibition *Black Male: Representations of Masculinity in Contemporary American Art* at the Whitney Museum of American Art, New York City. This work, considered a linchpin in discourse around identity politics in artistic practice, now forms part of the Tate collection.

Born in 1965 in the Bronx, New York, Harris was raised in Dar es Salaam, Tanzania, and in New York City. In the following interview, Harris recalls how photography was part of his upbringing, which in many respects accounts for his intuitive understanding of how images shape our understanding of society, history and culture. Working predominantly with photographic images spanning four decades, Harris has continually sought ways to reimagine how the medium is used, incorporating it into various media and performances.

After *Constructs #10 – #13* Harris continued to explore studio-based photography in several series. *The Watering Hole* 1996 constitutes his initial engagement with collage and montage, a nine-panel work in which he photographed personal ephemera juxtaposed with media representations based on research materials compiled over a five-year period following the first news reports on serial killer Jeffrey Dahmer. Representing a complex portrayal of desire, race, death and the media, this key work foreshadows an approach that would come to inform Harris's subsequent series, such as Blow Up (2004–10) and the

Shadow Works (2017–20), in which he would integrate his photography with source materials from his research and personal ephemera into site-specific collages, photographic montages and assemblages.

Harris also works as a photojournalist. In contrast to his studio practice, Harris's documentary photography demonstrates his eye for detail as well as the dialogic connection that he forms with portrait subjects. These qualities are exemplified in Harris's Ghana series (2008–10), which he produced while residing there over a seven-year period as a Professor of Art with New York University's Global programme in Accra. His photographs documenting the local queer community have come to take on renewed significance in light of Ghana's draconian legislation criminalising people identifying as LGBTQIA+ as well as those who promote or support their equal rights.

Community and history is the focal point of Harris's Ektachrome Archive, comprised of an extensive personal collection of 35mm Ektachrome colour reversal slides documenting his life circa late 1980s through the early 2000s. Featuring many notable figures such as Nan Goldin, Stuart Hall, Essex Hemphill, Catherine Opie, Marlon Riggs and Christina Sharpe, who continue to influence discourses around art, identity and politics, Ektachrome Archive serves as a living documentary testament to the expressive power of life fully lived.

Throughout his works, Harris's use of layering – both material and metaphorical – finds its apotheosis in his Shadow Works. These framed assemblages contain photographic dye sublimation prints of studio-wall collages composed of images of his earlier artworks, news clippings and ephemera, inset against Ghanaian fabrics, some appended with the artist's personal objects. In contrast to Harris's site-specific collages and installations in which photographic images often proliferate across the gallery wall, these assemblages rely on framing, thus intensifying the impact of each singular constellation whose often recurring imagery and material elements visually engage viewers through their resonant multiplicity. Harris's Shadow Works demonstrate the artist's ability to fuse the personal with the political through a network of visual forms that interact with each other, much like they increasingly do throughout our everyday contemporary lives.

Fiontán Moran
Curator, International Art, Tate

LYLE ASHTON HARRIS AND FIONTÁN MORAN IN CONVERSATION

FM I read that your grandfather had a keen interest in photography, so was it always an important part of your life?

LAH Cameras were always present in my family – James Van Der Zee photographed my grandparents' wedding portrait. The invitation card for my first New York exhibition at Jack Tilton Gallery in 1994 was a photograph of me taken by my late cousin, Ricky PJ. My grandfather took thousands of Ektachrome slides on his Leica CL camera documenting his family and community in depth – I recall being photographed by him a lot while I was growing up! He also shot Super 8 films and produced video recordings using early consumer cameras. It wasn't until I fully encountered the extent of his archive that I became aware of the material scope of his work, which includes a series of recorded appearances by Black people on television in the late twentieth century. Our family library also contained a great collection of photobooks, like Roy DeCarava's *The Sweet Flypaper of Life* 1955 and Ernest Cole's *House of Bondage* 1967. Ernest had been acquainted with my family through my South African stepfather Pule Leinaeng (also a photographer), as both of them were involved with the anti-apartheid exile community in New York.

FM Was there an understanding of how these photographs contributed to a broader dialogue around representation?

LAH My grandfather was a 'race man' and a disciple of W.E.B. Du Bois, so there was a deep understanding of culture and history. But I don't think people were sitting around in armchairs discussing it – they were just living their lives deeply engaged in their community [with an] understanding of being both an architect and contributor to that culture.

FM From the beginning of your practice, you foregrounded questions of race, gender and sexuality in your work. Did you always have an innate confidence in exploring this subject matter?

LAH It's not a choice to be gay, but it is a choice about your level of embodiment. I've always been fascinated by how people like Pier Paolo

Pasolini or Isaac Julien or Derek Jarman or Marlon Riggs made those choices. Thinking back to the opening of the *Black Male* exhibition at the Whitney Museum in 1994 (when *Constructs* – now in the Tate collection – was showing), at the opening I wore a one-piece, sleeveless tuxedo with something diaphanous underneath – a type of embodiment upsetting bourgeois notions of decorum. The choice to radically insist on that embodiment and with that to negotiate multiple spaces – it was my anointing. It can be hard to explain to younger generations – there was something radical about that embodiment and the cost of being out in the way that I was at the time.

FM Was *Constructs* always engineered to create a rupture?

LAH I think it's more about my internal working process, and secondarily it suggests a rupture. Given the constraints of society, I think queer people can over-police their desire which produces a double consciousness.

Before the *Black Male* exhibition, while I was studying at CalArts, a rupture actually happened when I presented an early prototype of *Constructs* in Allan Sekula's graduate photography seminar. In that early version, the silhouette of my figure with my arms akimbo is cut out from the printed photo over which I had written 'Faggot' in red lipstick. And that was the work. At the time it meant a lot to go into a classroom and queer that space.

FM The essays in the *Black Male* catalogue frame *Constructs* in relation to Mapplethorpe's images of naked Black men. Was that always the original intention behind the work?

LAH At the time, Mapplethorpe's photographs were considered as definitive images of Black men. So with anyone else who was working with that subject there would be an inevitable comparison – not as a way to open up dialogue, but to close it down! The fact is, at a certain point in contemporary image culture Mapplethorpe was both dominant *and* transgressive. So I've had to wrestle with his work, becoming versed in the critical literature around it. Similarly, Tom of Finland – whose work I really, really love! Beyond the racialised desire in his works, I also felt drawn to other forms of representation in the history of photography, or painting, or art history – such as the work of George Platt Lynes, which for me is even more radical and interesting because the men were not as aestheticised. I can't overstate how critical it has been to have today's photographic canon expanded through voices such as Ajamu X, John Edmonds, Clifford Prince King and Paul Mpagi Sepuya.

FM Rather than working with a friend or a model, did you use your own body because it was something you were personally working through?

LAH For me it was about wrestling with representation through my own embodiment using a certain type of performative gesture to challenge binary notions around the body and expand its possibilities. My friend the Black gay poet Essex Hemphill described my work as experiments, because I couldn't know what would result until I was actually doing it. And for me there was also a kind of exorcism that came through that process.

FM I've often thought about *Constructs* in relation to a history of artists using photography as a space to perform, to create alternative selves. This sense of theatricality is also conveyed by the way they were printed life-size and, originally, pinned to the wall so that you became more aware of the physicality of the photograph as an object. Was performance something that you considered in the making of these works or was it more intuitive?

LAH All of that is there, but I don't really think of it that way. I see it more as a distillation of one's life in developing an understanding of embodiment, being out and queer, as well as a certain engagement with cultural history. It's connected to me discovering the word 'faggot' in a James Baldwin book that my mother was reading, then later being called that as a slur during junior high school in the Bronx, and the social pressure to control my unique self-expression, which was viewed by my peers as effeminate. That early work came out of my interest in exploring the power of gesture. The skirt I wore in *Construct #10* was just a piece of crinoline fabric that I had in my studio. In 1985 I had visited my brother Thomas Allen Harris in Amsterdam, where androgyny was big, and I also found inspiration in what Grace Jones was doing at the time. Performativity was certainly intentional in *Brotherhood, Crossroads and Etcetera*, a photographic collaboration with Thomas that we shot in 1994 against a backdrop of tricolors from the UNIA Pan-African flag, which had its roots in our having lived in Tanzania for several years while growing up, where there was an established community of African-Americans seeking to pursue a utopian ideal in having emigrated back to Africa.

FM So while there's a theatrical element there, it's really about the process of dealing with those forms of oppression and the difficulty of navigating the world.

LAH It's also about the triumph of having succeeded, of being 'out' and of saying the abuse stops here – the triumph of 'talking back', in the spirit of bell hooks and claiming my queerness.[1] While we know of countless people who have died, who have been killed, it's not only about trauma. I think it's important to talk about the triumph of laying claim to an experience and rechannelling its energy into creative expression that will go back out into the culture where an intergenerational transmission can take place. In a public conversation in 2023 with Kehinde Wiley at the Guggenheim Museum in New York, he recalled first seeing *Constructs* in the *Black Male* exhibition and the impact that it made on him as a teenager by portraying a different sense of self that might be possible. So it's not simply about self-expression, but also about focusing that energy, developing a space in which to be seen, and producing reverberations into the wider culture.

FM This idea of transmission and reverberations reminds me of how the curator Okwui Enwezor described photography in your *Excessive Exposure* monograph as something that is constantly referring to a past and to a present and implicit within that is a future.[2] Were there any indications of the significance of *Constructs* when you first publicly exhibited them at Camerawork in 1990?

LAH It's important to acknowledge the circumstances in which *Constructs* were produced. Growing up in the Bronx and then living in Tanzania, I had not been spending much time in New York City when AIDS began making news in the 1980s. My early life was circumscribed by family and then later university, where I became actively engaged but largely within the confines of academia. Although I had been raised in a family whose Black activist commitments spanned the Civil Rights movement to the anti-apartheid struggles of the African National Congress, my temperament and training is more in the realm of aesthetics.

I arrived at CalArts for grad school in 1988 at the onset of second-wave AIDS activism, which moved in two complementary directions: one was concerned with finding effective ways to support afflicted communities such as GMHC (Gay Men's Health Crisis) and devising direct actions such as AIDS Coalition to Unleash Power (ACT UP); the other was concerned with finding new ways to deploy aesthetics to create alternative or queer spaces. *Constructs*, which I photographed in 1989 while I was at CalArts, came out of that dynamic at a time when queer activism had become much more radical. I found encouragement in this from my professor John Greyson, who introduced his students to cutting-edge film and queer theory, championing the creative efforts of contemporaries such as Tom Kalin and Gregg Bordowitz among others.

Constructs represented a clearing, an in-between space in which to radicalise queer self-expression for me and for others at a time of much academic debate around identity and pornography and its relation to anti-aesthetics, post-studio practice and post-structuralism.

Having previously met John Akomfrah, Martina Attille, Sonia Boyce and Isaac Julien while I was studying at CalArts, when I arrived in London for the initial public showing of *Constructs* in the *Autoportraits* group exhibition at Camerawork in 1990, I found a welcoming reception from Sunil Gupta and Stuart Hall.[3] This proved to be a pivotal moment for me, in which I forged generative connections with a very formidable group of contemporary Black British intellectuals who were deeply political and deeply embodied. Soon after, a black-and-white photograph titled *Man and Woman #1* from my Americas series (1987–8) was featured on the cover of the critical British photography magazine *Ten.8* in 1991, as well as on the cover of the international literary journal *Transition*, published in 1992 (which had recently been re-launched by scholars Henry Louis Gates Jr, Kwame Anthony Appiah and Wole Soyinka), and included Adrian Piper's seminal essay 'Passing for White, Passing for Black'.

FM Could you talk about how your work relates to ideas of performance?

LAH It's interesting because while the performative gesture was in my work since the mid-1980s [and I knew] how to compact the energy and to survive, there was a cost in that and a deep, deep fear. When I did my first public performance of *Performing MJ* in 2006, it laid bare a deeper transgression connected to ideas of the grotesque and confronting the audience that came out of years of self-censoring.

FM Why did you decide that work had to be a performance rather than a photograph or installation?

LAH That performance was initially presented in 2004 for an academic conference held at Yale titled *Regarding Michael Jackson: Performing Racial, Gender, and Sexual Difference Center Stage* organised by Uri McMillan and Seth Clark Silberman.[4] A few weeks prior, I had seen a play that portrayed the killing of a South Asian *hijra*, a cross-dressing 'third gender' figure. As a result, I found myself shutting down – a literal collapse – which also represented my belated emotional processing of a series of disturbing news items. These included reports on the heinous sexual abuse of a Black gay man while serving time in prison on tax evasion charges, as well as the highly publicised trial resulting in the conviction and sentencing of Jamal Michael Barrow (aka Shyne) to a decade in prison, for which it's believed he took the fall for Sean 'Diddy' Combs, who was acquitted on related gun possession charges in connection with a 1999 shooting in a New York nightclub. I found all that to be highly triggering, but it put me in touch with my own trauma from my childhood and early adolescence and informed my insight into a Black public figure such as Michael Jackson. Through its performative embodiment, my sense of vulnerability got infused and 'enfleshed' in *Performing MJ*, which can also be seen as an organic outgrowth of my 20 x 24 Polaroid of performative self-portraits of Billie Holiday and Josephine Baker, as well as my two series Memoirs of Hadrian (2002) and Better Days (2002).[5]

FM Your work *The Watering Hole* from 1996 was the beginning of you moving away from a posed studio setup to something more exploratory. It examines the relationship between serial killer Jeffrey Dahmer and broader ideas around the media representation of Black men and desire through a range of source materials – photographs, magazine articles, clippings and handwritten notes. Did that emerge from a desire to break out of the limits of the singular series of images, or was it connected to something else?

LAH It wasn't so much having exhausted what a portrait or a self-portrait could do, but a way to complicate and flesh out a deeper understanding of what that could be. I was trying to develop something that dealt with a multiplicity of ideas and to have the work itself bear the complexity of that thinking.

My development of *The Watering Hole* was impacted by having encountered the transgressive photographs and performances of artists Bob Flanagan and Sheree Rose, who were part of the BDSM scene in Los Angeles when I lived there in the late 1980s and early 1990s. I was drawn to their degree of vulnerability in testing the limits of embodiment. Initially the series was intended to be presented as a collage on wood panelling, but at studio visits I noticed that viewers were inevitably drawn towards its less challenging material. It was clear that certain elements needed to be amplified. So I decided to re-photograph the collages in order to redirect the viewer's gaze. *The Watering Hole* was about laying bare the complexities of life, the complexities of desire, and part of its charge is that it's anti-compartmentalised, asking what it means to bring all these ambivalent desires and complexities together in a single framing.

FM Is desire an important part of your work?

LAH Definitely – desire in relationship to knowledge, to the erotic, to giving skin, to those things that are unspoken, to memory, to finding interconnected tissues between the past and the present.

FM Desire and looking being so intertwined.

LAH There's a difference between just looking and then capturing the looking, because that's where the intentionality comes in. Everyone's looking. People are looking and then shutting down. Or people are looking and then opening up. But the idea of mapping the looking is part of the genesis of my work.

FM At the time did people find *The Watering Hole* challenging?

LAH Given where we were then historically – the Black Popular Culture conference at the Studio Museum in Harlem and the DIA Center for the Arts in New York had taken place in 1991 and the art world was just starting to consider culture as a site about which to think theoretically – something was happening! Still, five years later in 1996, *The Watering Hole* was seen as destabilising given that it did not feel like safe subject matter – not only the subject of Jeffrey Dahmer, a particular figure who literally consumed young Black men, but also the fact that *Ebony* magazine wasn't reporting on it. That work was considered very difficult, asking people to look at their complicity in the consumption of the 'other' and how we're all implicated in a system of desire, including myself. It's one thing to read about Dahmer in the newspaper, but quite another to serve it up at a gallery walk-through with afternoon tea, showing people the interconnectedness around that. And because my first solo exhibition, *The Good Life* – which was presented at Jack Tilton's

New York gallery in 1994 – had included lush, large-format Polaroids that viewers were drawn to, I can remember Jack asking, 'Where's the winning image?'

FM In the 1990s you did some portraits of well-known figures for magazines, but in 2001 you began to do more documentary photography, first in Italy and then Ghana. Could you talk about how this relates to the works that are more research-led and studio-based?

LAH My studio-based work, photojournalism and vernacular photography all feed each other. The *calcio* photographs were shot during my fellowship at the American Academy in Rome. I had read a cover story in the *International Herald Tribune* on racism and antisemitism in European football, so I proposed a story to *The New York Times Magazine* on soccer 'hooligans' and Black players that was inspired by a previous feature juxtaposing South African perpetrators of apartheid with its victims. While shooting on the playing field in stadiums, I became fascinated by the crowds of frenzied spectators during the game. As a result of my research for that shoot, I came across an Adidas advert that featured the famous footballer Zinedine Zidane receiving a pedicure from a Black man, which led to the development of my Blow Up installation series. While in Ghana, the dialogic relationship between different ways of looking continued to evolve in my work.

FM The time and research you've done on Ghana has culminated with you co-editing the Fall 2023 issue of the photography magazine *Aperture*.

LAH This was the first time I undertook serving in an editorial capacity, in this case as co-editor with Nii Obodai, a Ghanaian photographer who's been a major force in that country's burgeoning art scene. After joining the Aperture Foundation's Board of Trustees in 2021, I became interested in the fact that one of its founders, the photographer Paul Strand, had visited Ghana at the invitation of its first president Kwame Nkrumah just as the country was making the transition to post-colonial independence. Given that *Aperture* had previously produced issues highlighting the photography coming out of major global cities, I thought it was timely to suggest an issue focused specifically on Accra. I'm particularly gratified that the issue we produced includes an article documenting the significance of safe queer spaces there, many of which no longer exist, and lays bare the current complexities around sexuality given the constraints wrought by increasing social conservatism globally.

FM Your current series Shadow Works that you've been working on since 2017 is a reflection on your time in Ghana, and it sees you return to the technique of photographing your collage materials and placing them in frames. Could you talk more about this?

LAH The Shadow Works assemblages relate to multiple ways of thinking about image-making and desire in a way that's more embedded. These works were prefigured by something Okwui Enwezor said to me in 2004, when he saw my site-specific installation *Blow Up I (Chicago)* at the Rhona Hoffman Gallery. He loved that work's energy and suggested I develop an appropriate framing device that could contain its 'combustion'. Serving as a kind of memento mori, the Shadow Works represent an outgrowth of my experiences living in Ghana over seven years. Inspired by Ghanaians' funerary use of printed textiles and Kente cloth, these works at once engage materially with the complicated personal, textual and erotic experiences that unfolded for me during the time I lived there. At the same time, the Shadow Works reflect a somewhat punk aesthetic that informed my work prior to living in Ghana, which by contrast can be rather formal.

FM This sense of reflection, and the line between the public and the private, is present in your Ektachrome Archive, which consists of a vast archive of images from the late 1980s and early 1990s. How did this work come about?

LAH Upon returning to the US in 2013, I found myself entering a grieving period, having ended a seven-year romantic relationship in Ghana. Around that same time, Isaac Julien contacted me to enquire about the documentary photographs I had shot while visiting London in 1991 for the *Autoportraits* exhibition at Camerawork and in 1995 for *Mirage: Enigmas of Race, Difference and Desire*, an exhibition and related conference on Frantz Fanon at the International Curators Forum curated by David A. Bailey. Isaac had expressed an interest in including some of those photos in his monograph *Isaac Julien: Riot*, which accompanied his MoMA exhibition *Ten Thousand Waves*. His enquiry led to my revisiting and excavating my archive of Ektachrome slides from those earlier years. Several of those images had been originally presented in my 1994 exhibition *The Good Life*, but the majority had never been widely shown. When I initially began publicly presenting these photos as slideshows – for example, at the Guggenheim Museum in New York for *Carrie Mae Weems LIVE* in 2015 – it was striking how these intimate portrayals evoking a recent past visibly moved viewers, prompting their open expression of emotion.

FM There's a joy seeing you and your community at work, at play and at rest in these images.

LAH It's interesting, because for me the satisfaction and joy in the Ektachrome Archive is more palpable when presented as an immersive installation with hanging projection screens and audio. I think one can easily get caught up in the nostalgia of many of those images; it was important to think it through so they felt fresh, considering the ways that photographs recirculate in both the past and the present to imagine a future.

FM Many of the people in those images – such as bell hooks, Marlon Riggs and Stuart Hall – have sadly passed away, yet their work and ideas continue to have relevance for a younger generation. Part of the sense of possibility in the work connects back to how you described *Constructs* as presenting a sense of hope or defiance. They're not about trauma or despair but about celebrating a right to exist.

LAH One thing we haven't brought up is the idea of service. What does it mean for embodiment to be a form of service, to push the language forward? Considering the initial reactions to the images in *Constructs* at the *Black Male* exhibition, then six years later in 2000 I'm getting commissions to photograph hip-hop legends such as Missy Elliott and dead prez for *Vibe* magazine – it shows how culture is always shifting.

FM I like the idea of serving – serving a look to serve a culture to serve the conversation and all the rest.

LAH I love that – not to be too absolute, because I think it's multivalent. We can take pleasure in that, experiencing the joy and freedom – maybe that's most immediate. But how that resonates and carries on is important in relation to continuing the service of a past generation that has not survived – Marlon Riggs, Essex Hemphill, Derek Jarman, David Wojnarowicz – but whose work has survived. What does it mean to actually expand on that carrying forward?

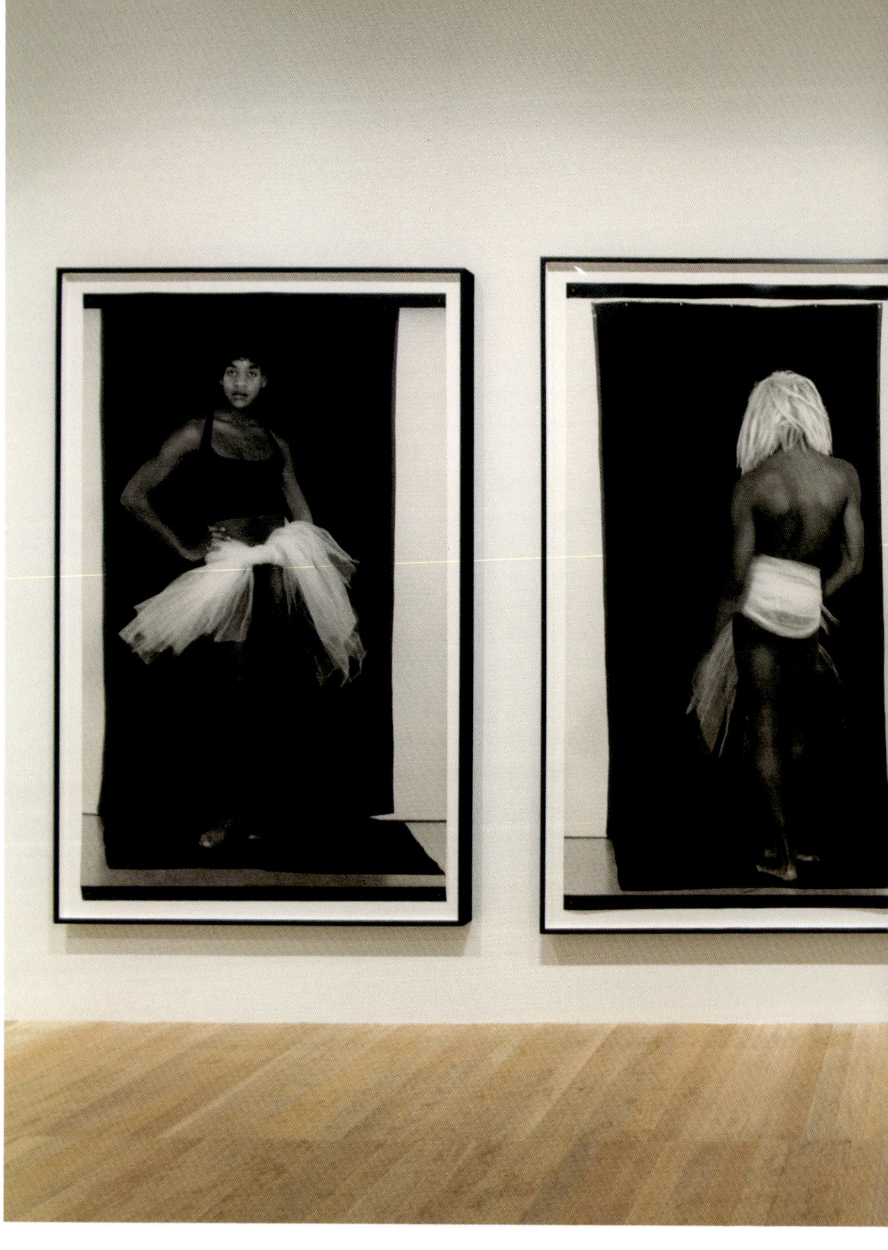

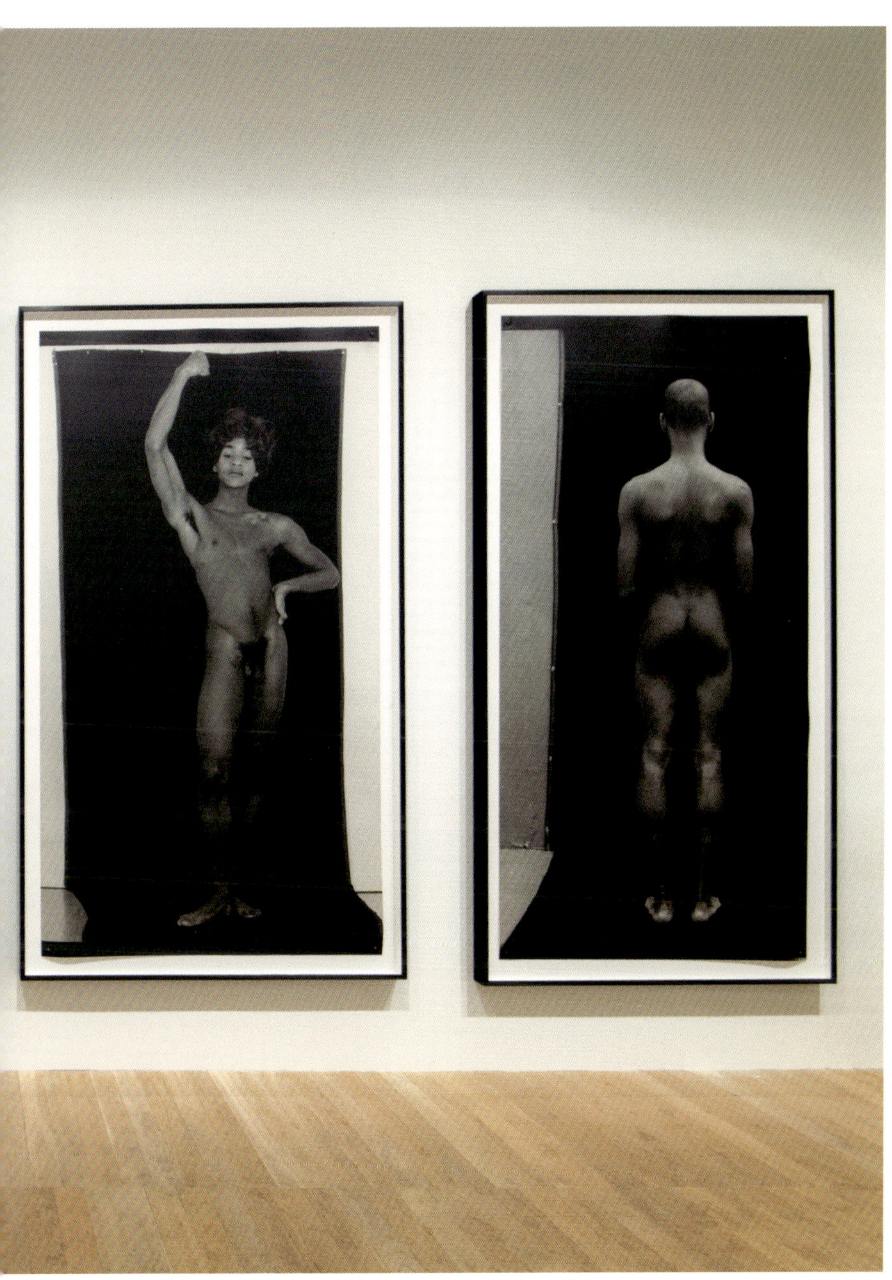

Constructs #10–#13 1989

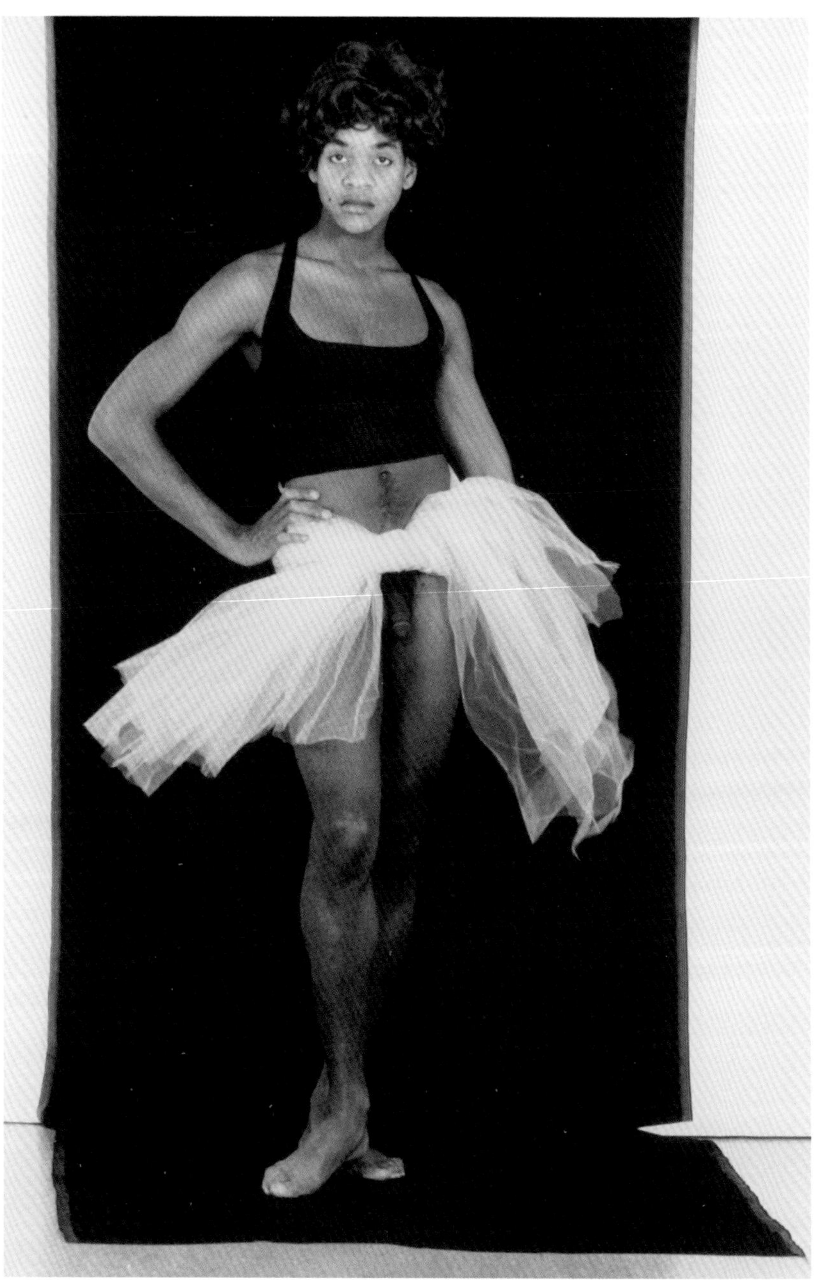

 Construct #10 1989

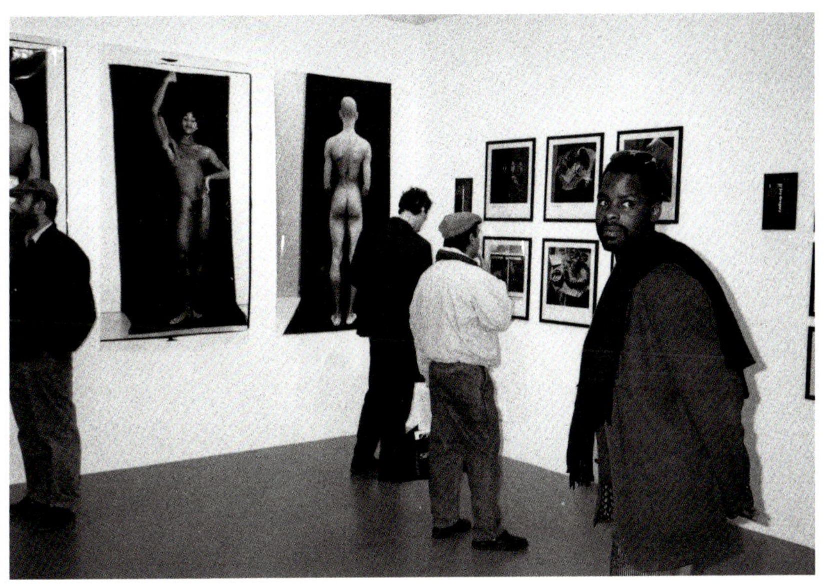

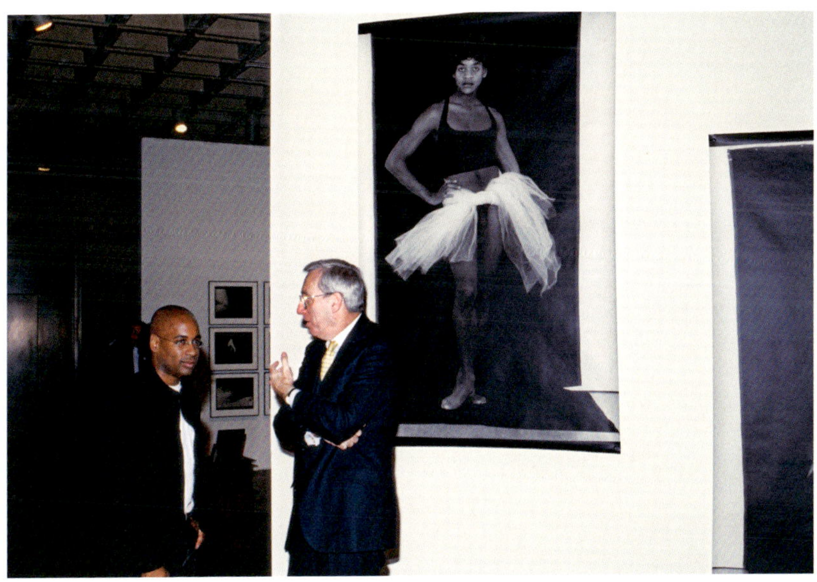

Top: David A. Bailey, *Autoportraits* exhibition, Camerawork, London, 1990
Bottom: *Glenn Ligon and Arthur Fleischer,* Black Male *exhibition opening, New York, 1994*
2015

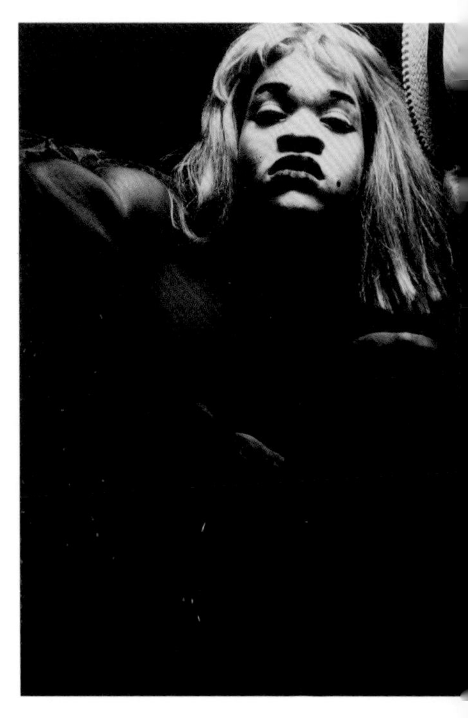

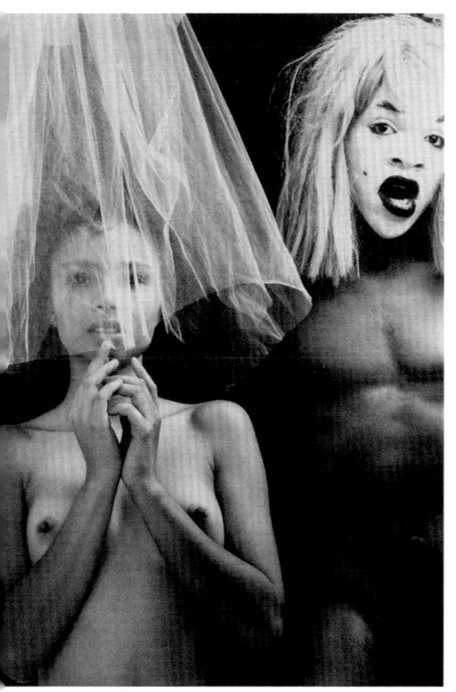

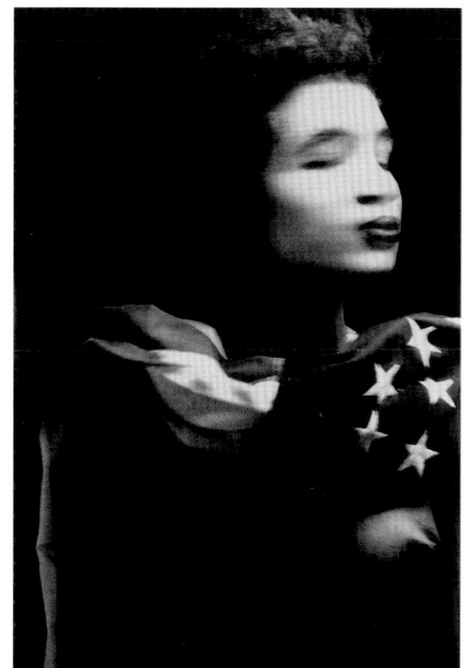

Americas (Triptych) [*Miss Girl*; *Kym, Lyle & Crinoline*; *Miss America*] 1987–8

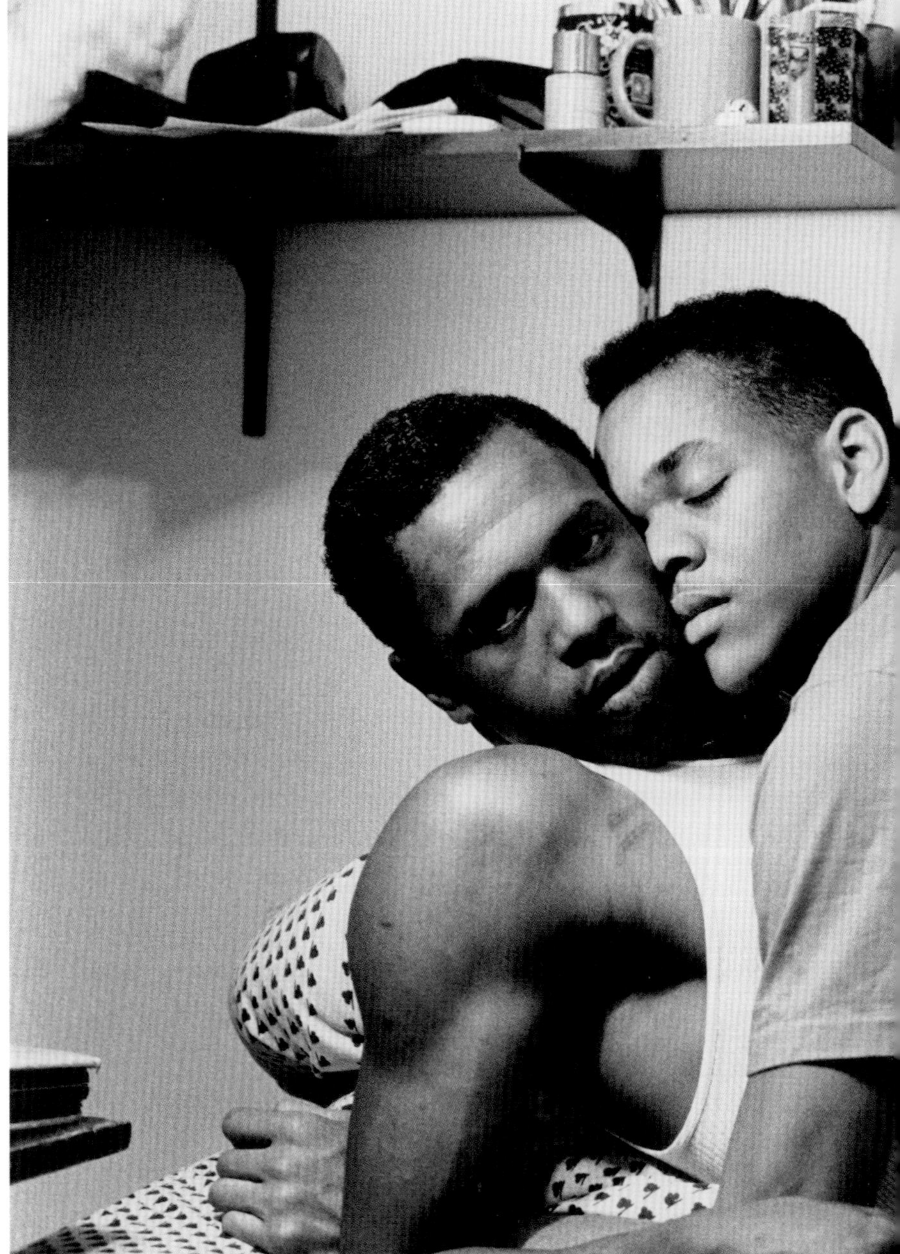

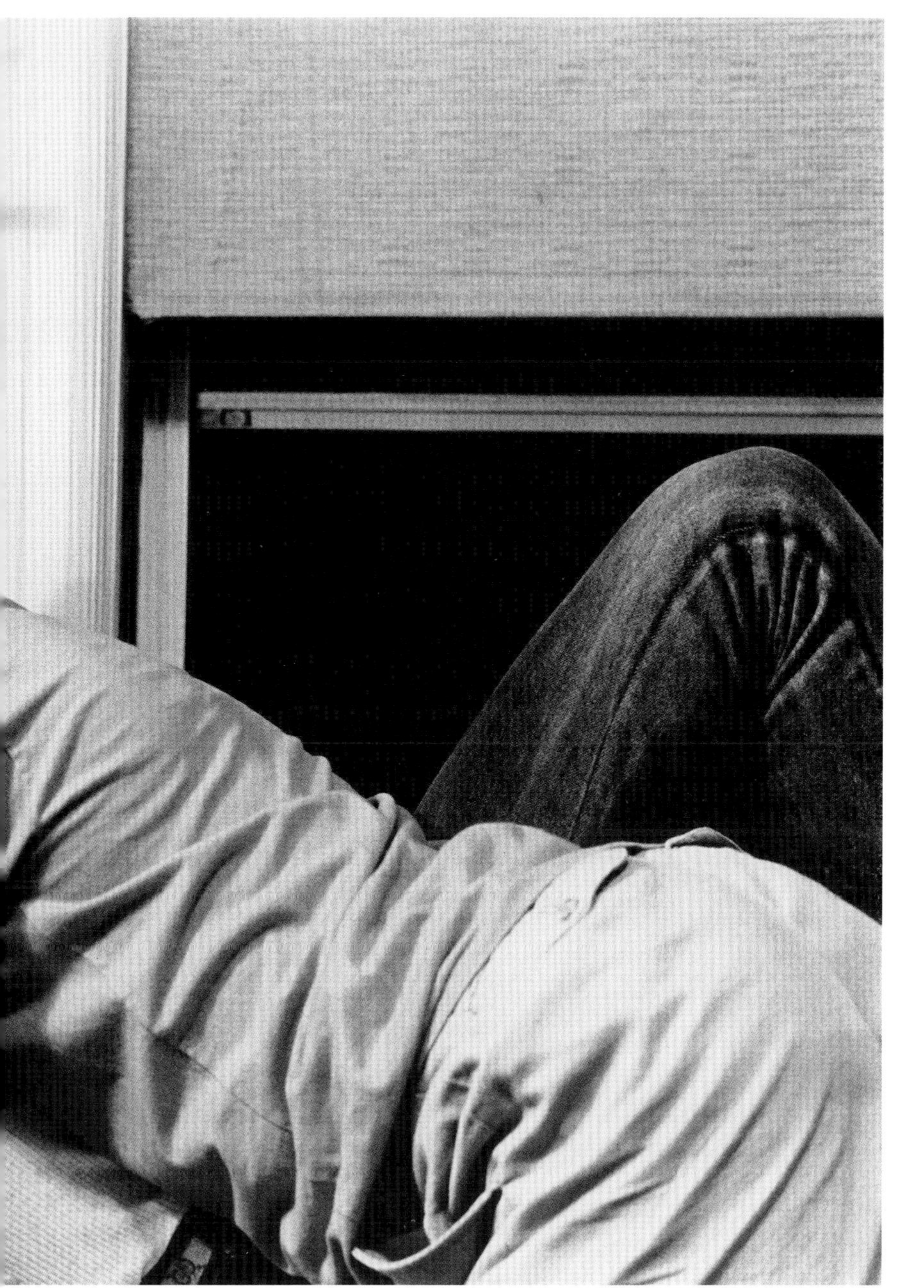

Untitled (*Lyle and Robert, Bronx, New York, circa mid-1980*s) 2022

Lyle by Thomas Munke (London, 1992) 2015

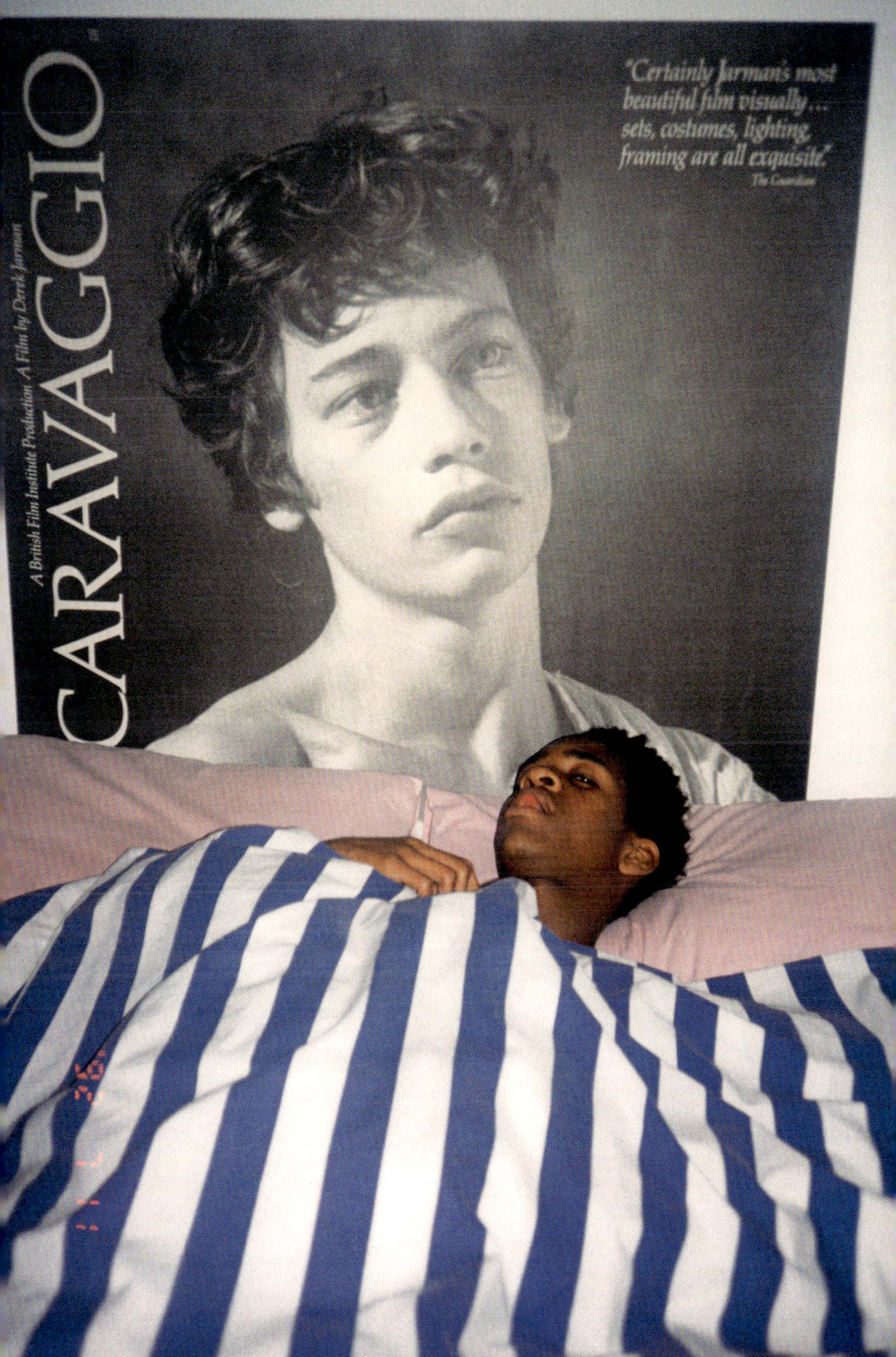
CARAVAGGIO
A British Film Institute Production A Film by Derek Jarman
"Certainly Jarman's most beautiful film visually… sets, costumes, lighting, framing are all exquisite."
The Guardian

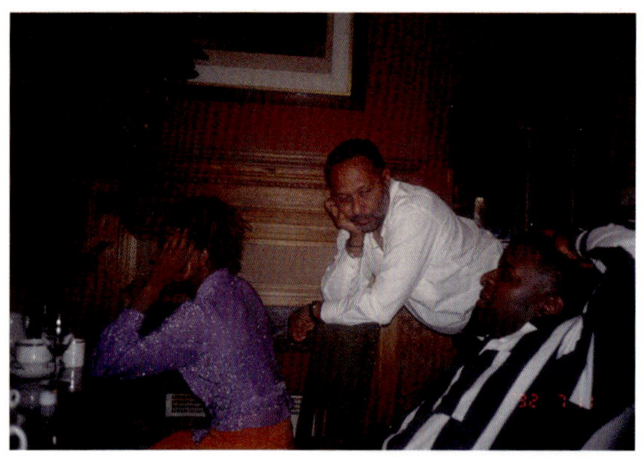

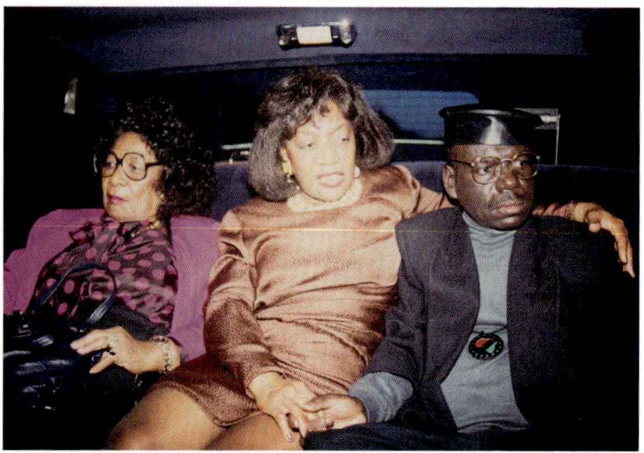

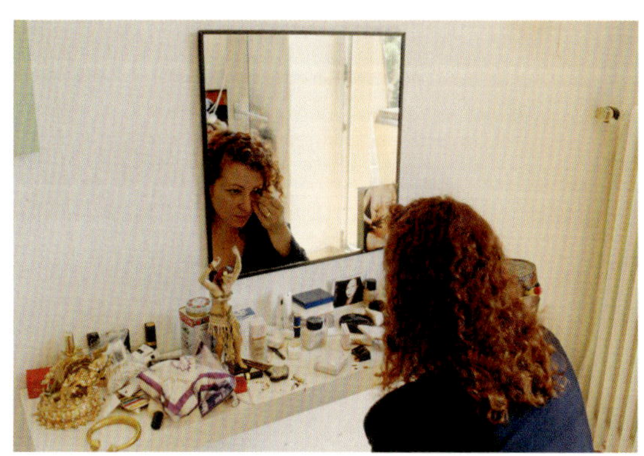

Top: *Sonia Boyce, Stuart Hall and Isaac Julien, 2 Brydges Place, Covent Garden, London, 1992* 2015
Middle: *Big Mama, Jean Riggs and Marlon Riggs (Berkeley, 1993)* 2018
Bottom: *Nan Goldin, Berlin, 1992* 2015

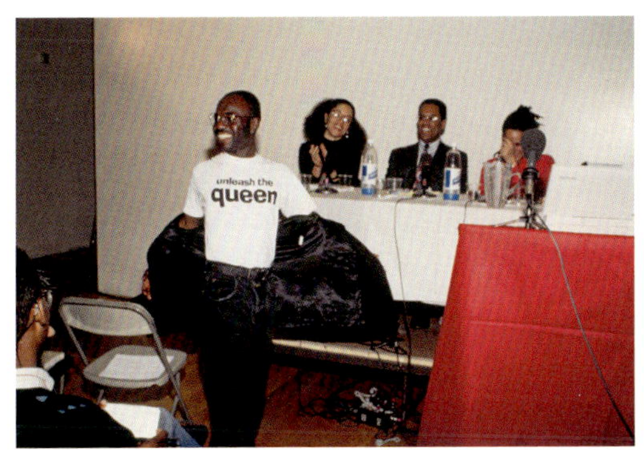

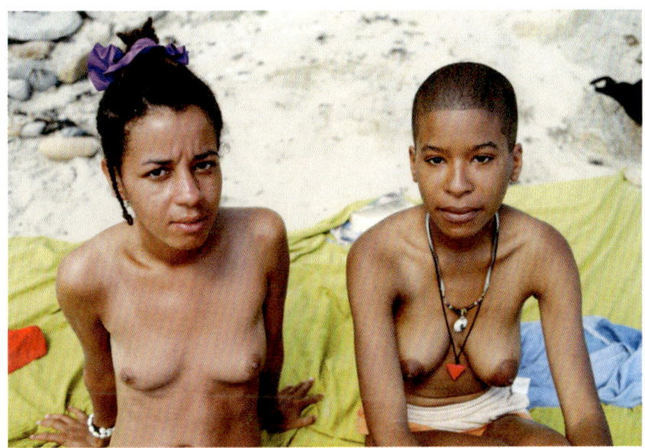

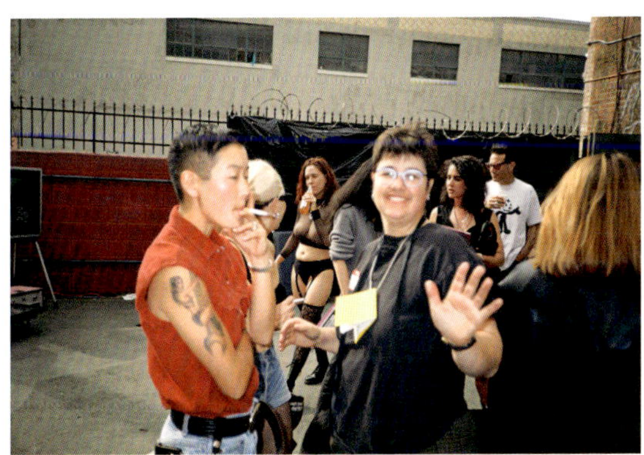

Top: *Marlon Riggs, Judith Wilson, Houston A. Baker, Jr. and Jacquie Jones at the Black Popular Culture Conference, (New York City, 1991)* 2016
Middle: *Lynne Mendes and Christina Sharpe at Gay Head/Aquinnah (Martha's Vineyard, late 1980s)* 2015
Bottom: *Jenny Shimizu and Catherine Opie at Sunset Junction Street Fair (Los Angeles,* early *1990s)* 2015

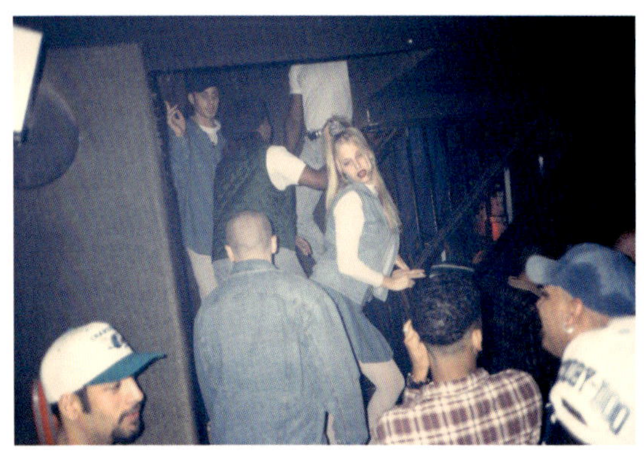

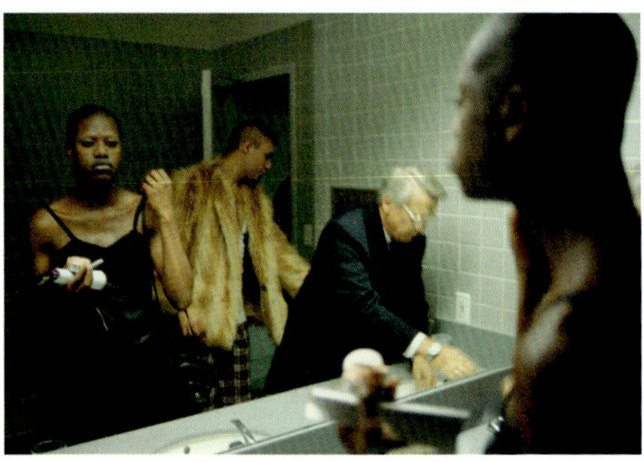

Top: *Nightlife (New York early 1990s)* 2015
Middle: *M. Lamar, Yerba Buena Center for the Arts, San Francisco, 1993* 2015
Bottom: Nightlife, London, 1992

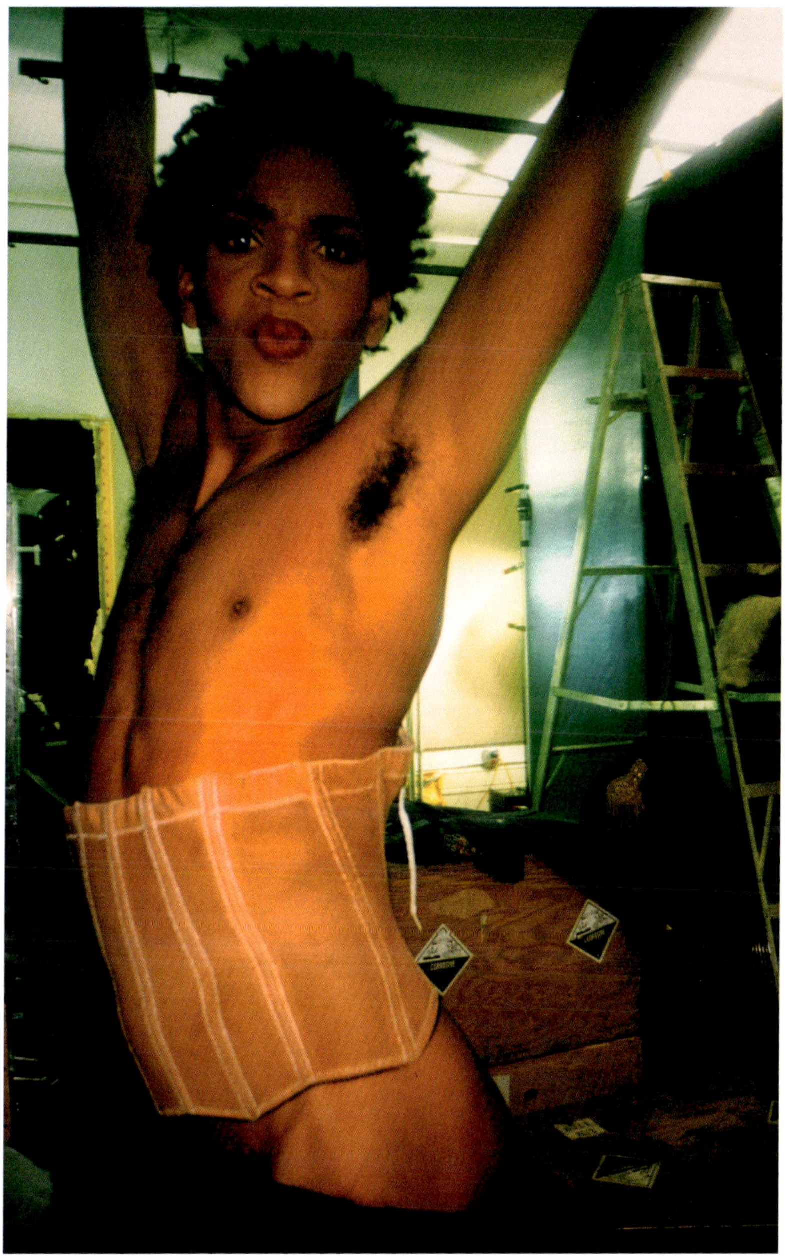

Vintage Lyle #2 (in collaboration with Margaret Nelson) 1994

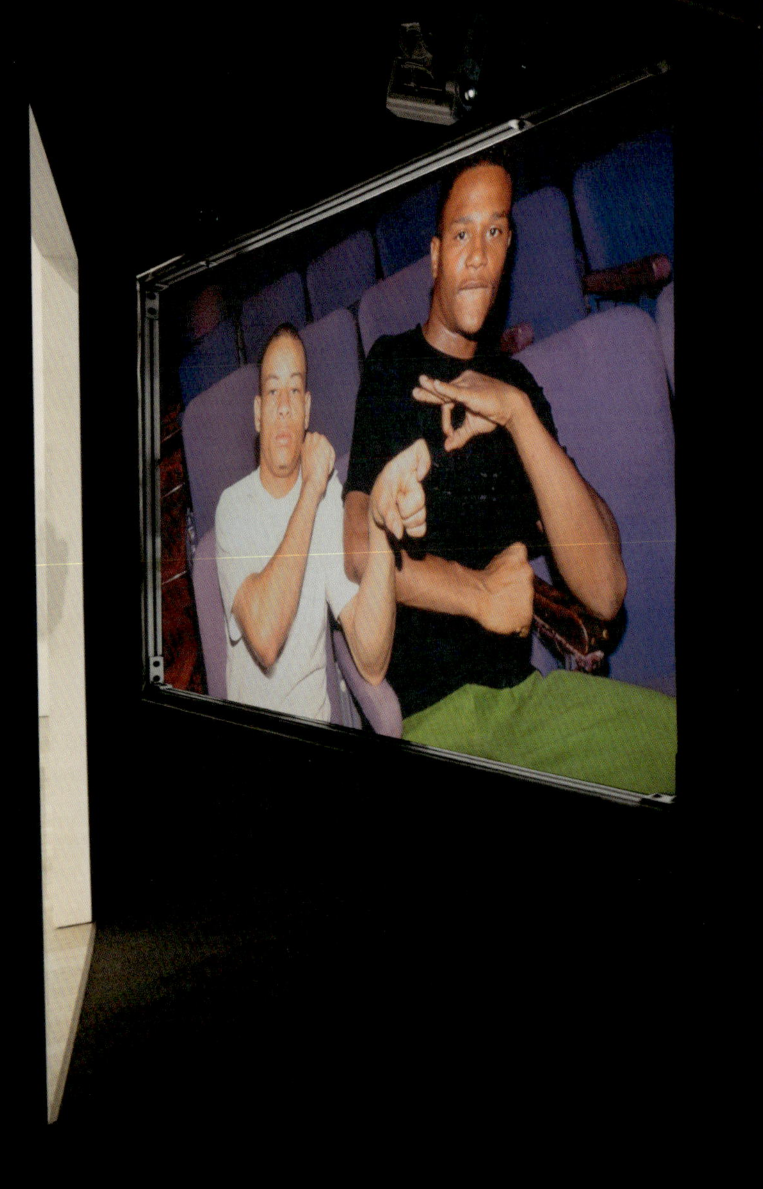

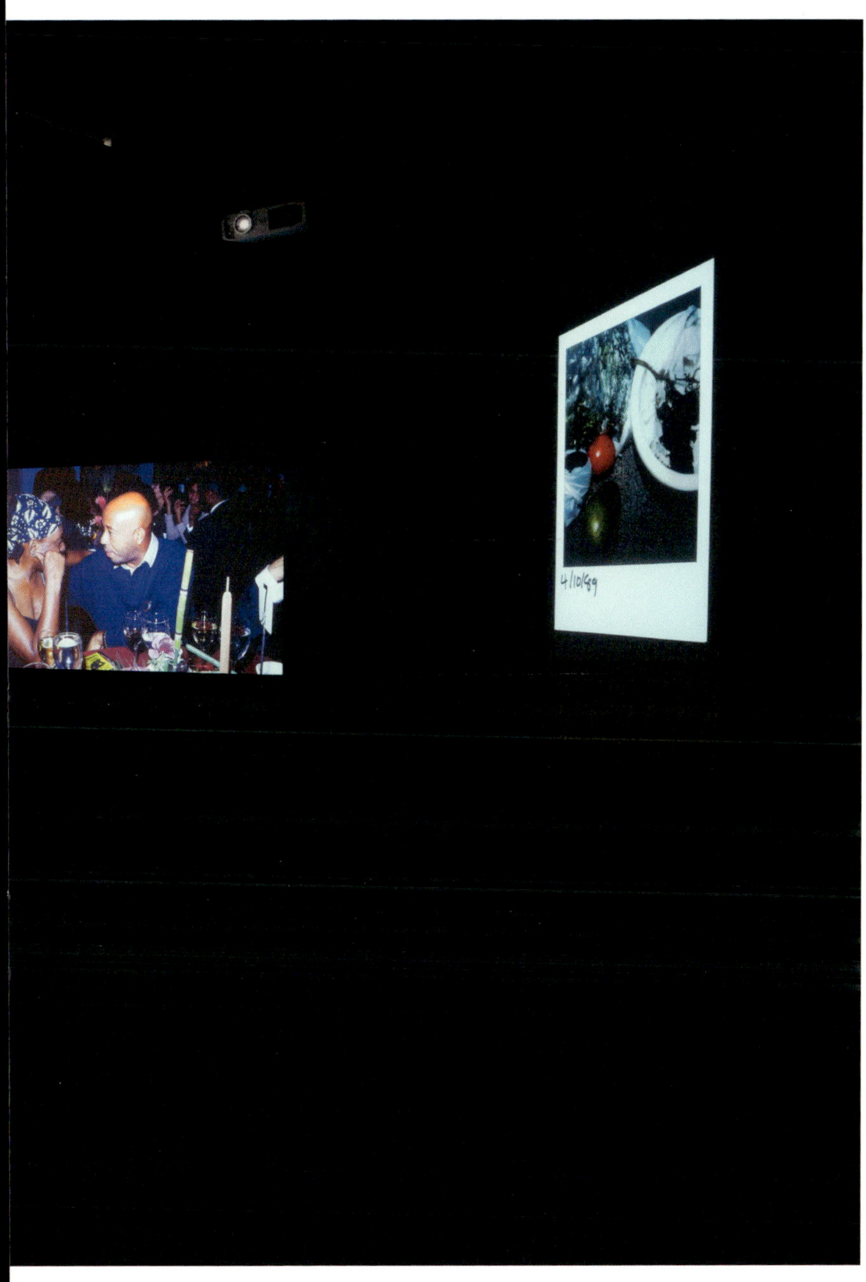

Ektachrome Archive (New York Mix), installation of *Once (Now) Again* at the Whitney Museum of American Art Biennial, 2017

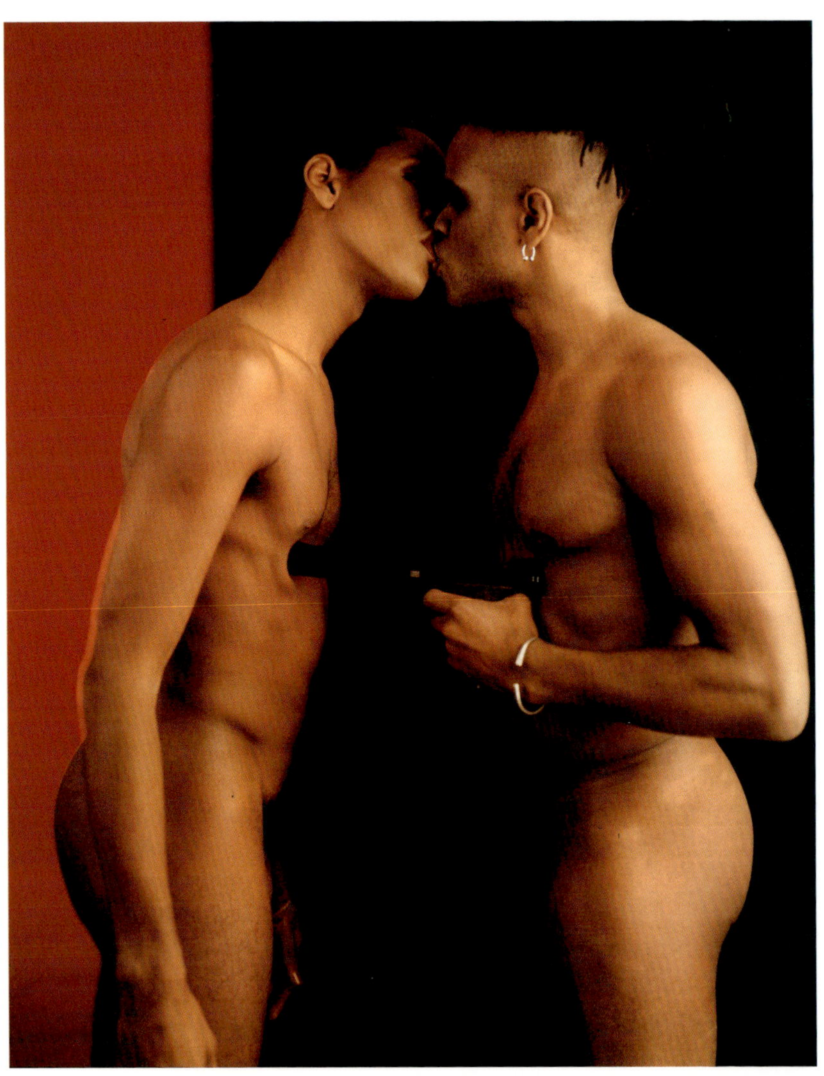

 Brotherhood, Crossroads and Etcetera #2 (in collaboration with Thomas Allen Harris) 1994

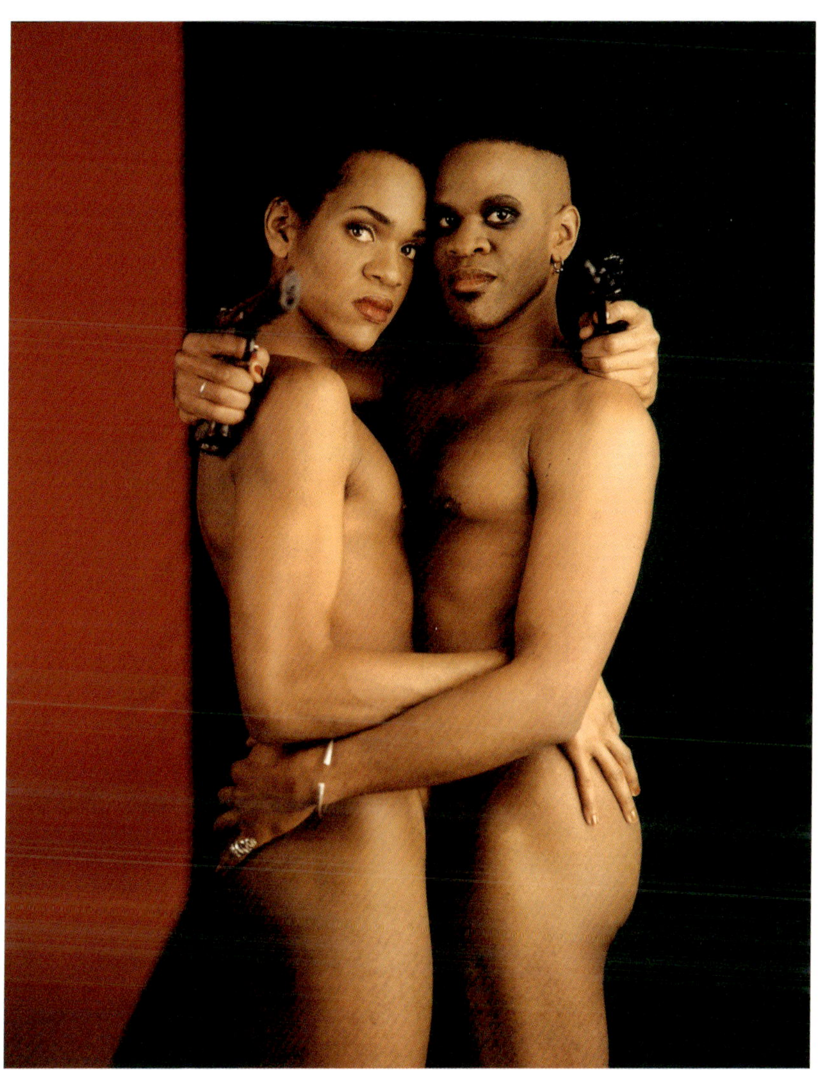

 Brotherhood, Crossroads and Etcetera #3 (in collaboration with Thomas Allen Harris) 1994

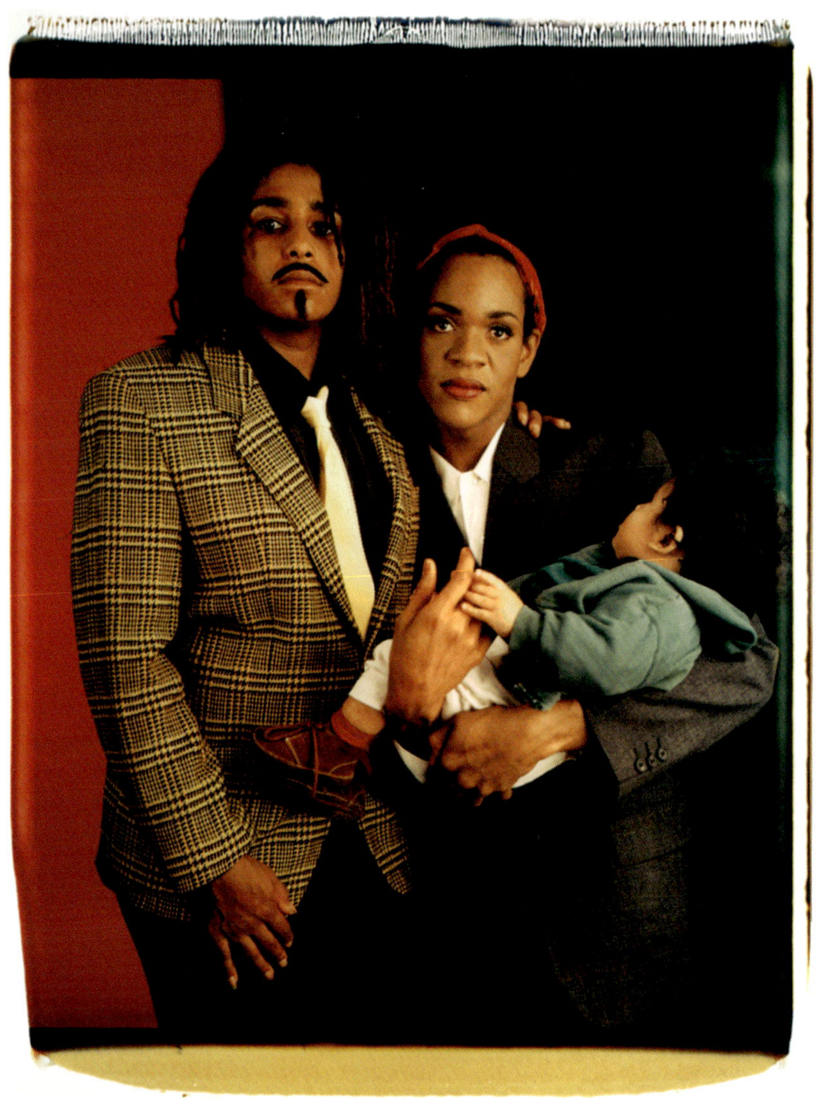

The Child 1994

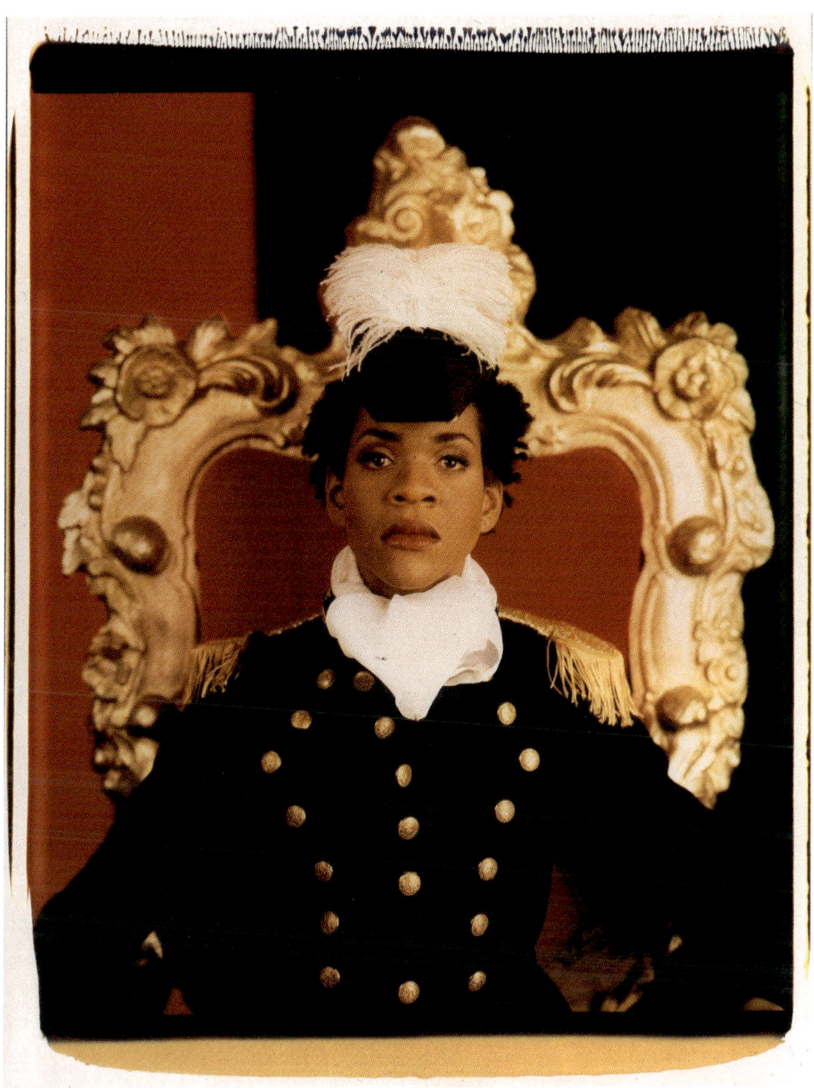

 Toussaint L'Ouverture 1994

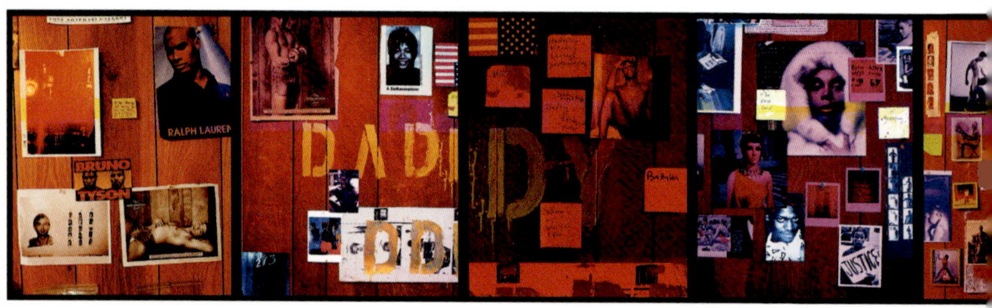
RALPH LAUREN
BRUNO
TYSON
DADDY
Babylon
JUSTICE 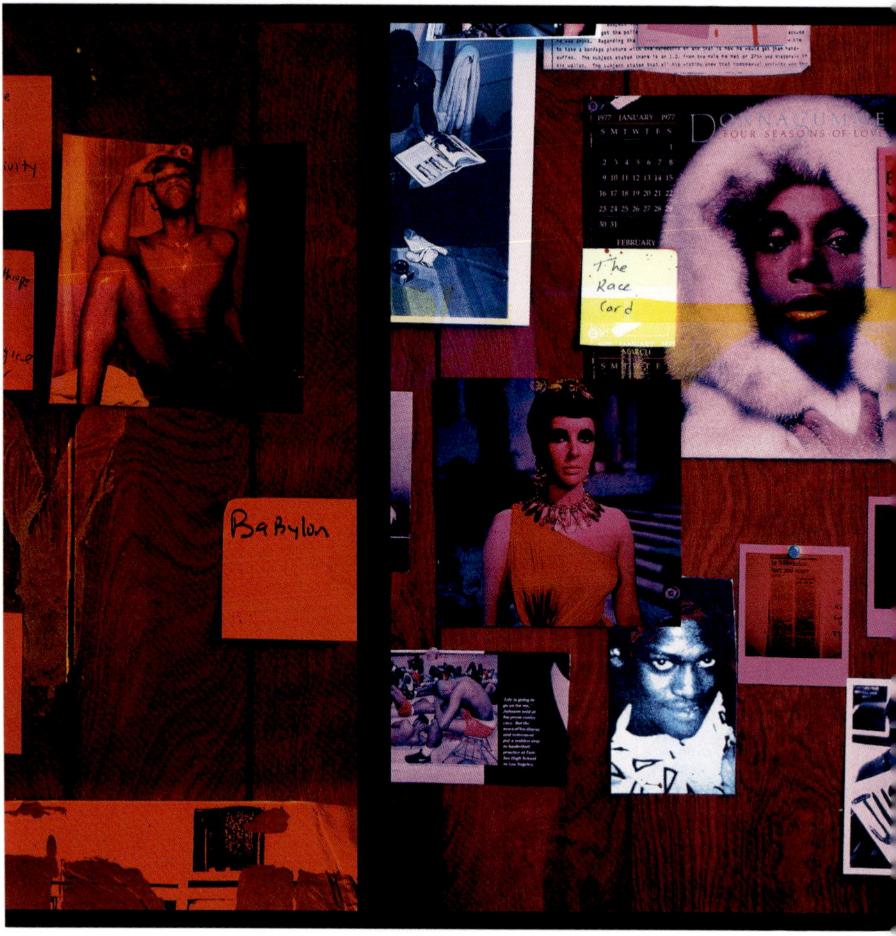
Babylon
The Race Card
1977 JANUARY 1977
FOUR SEASONS OF LOVE
FEBRUARY

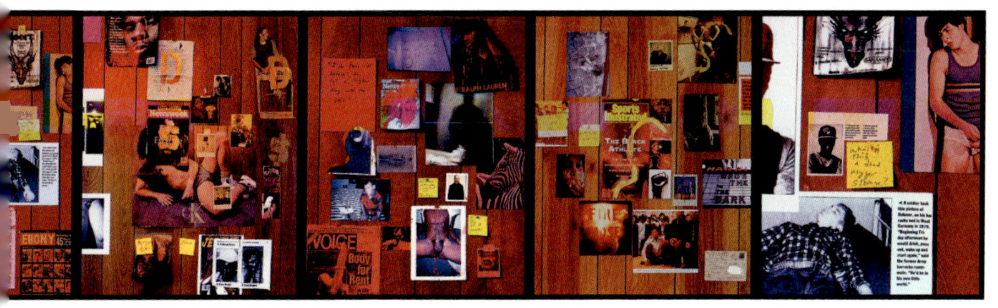

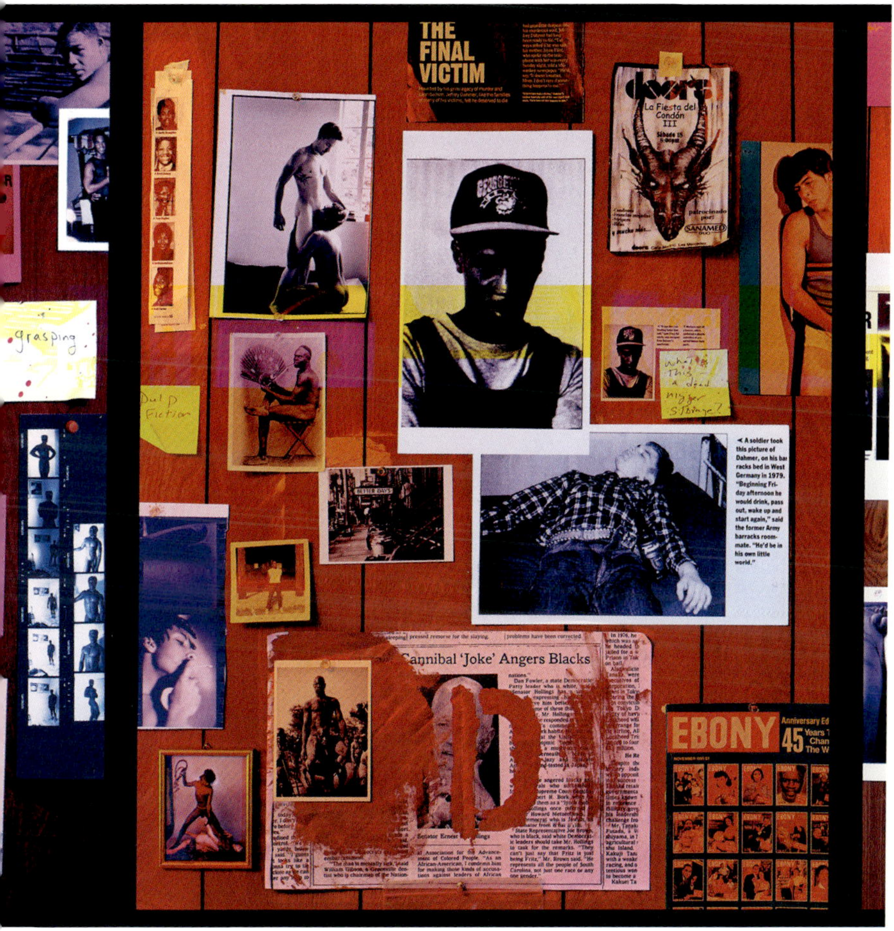

Top: *The Watering Hole I–IX* 1996
Bottom: *The Watering Hole VII, III, VIII* 1996 (detail)

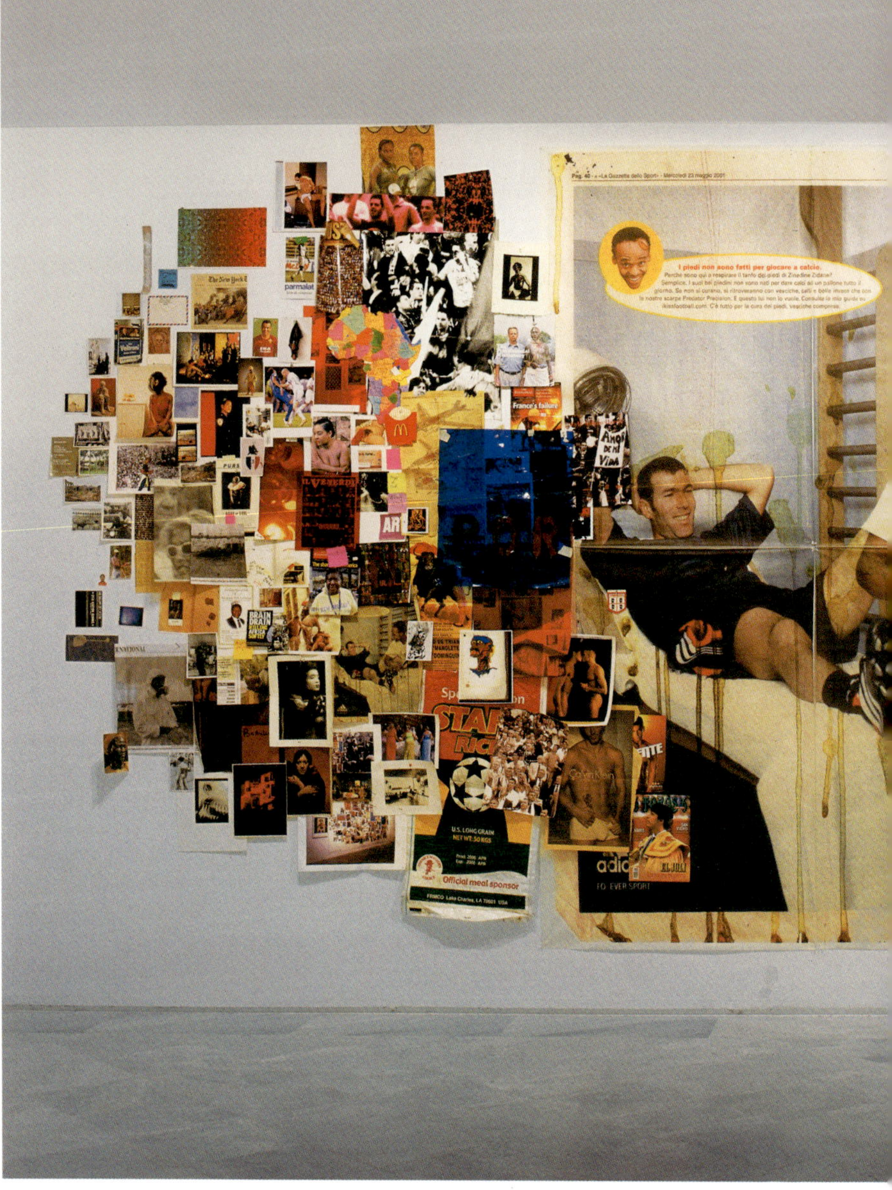

I piedi non sono fatti per giocare a calcio.
parmalat
The New York T
France's failure
AMOR DE MI VIDA
BRAIN DRAIN
ART
Official meal sponsor
U.S. LONG GRAIN
Calvin Klein

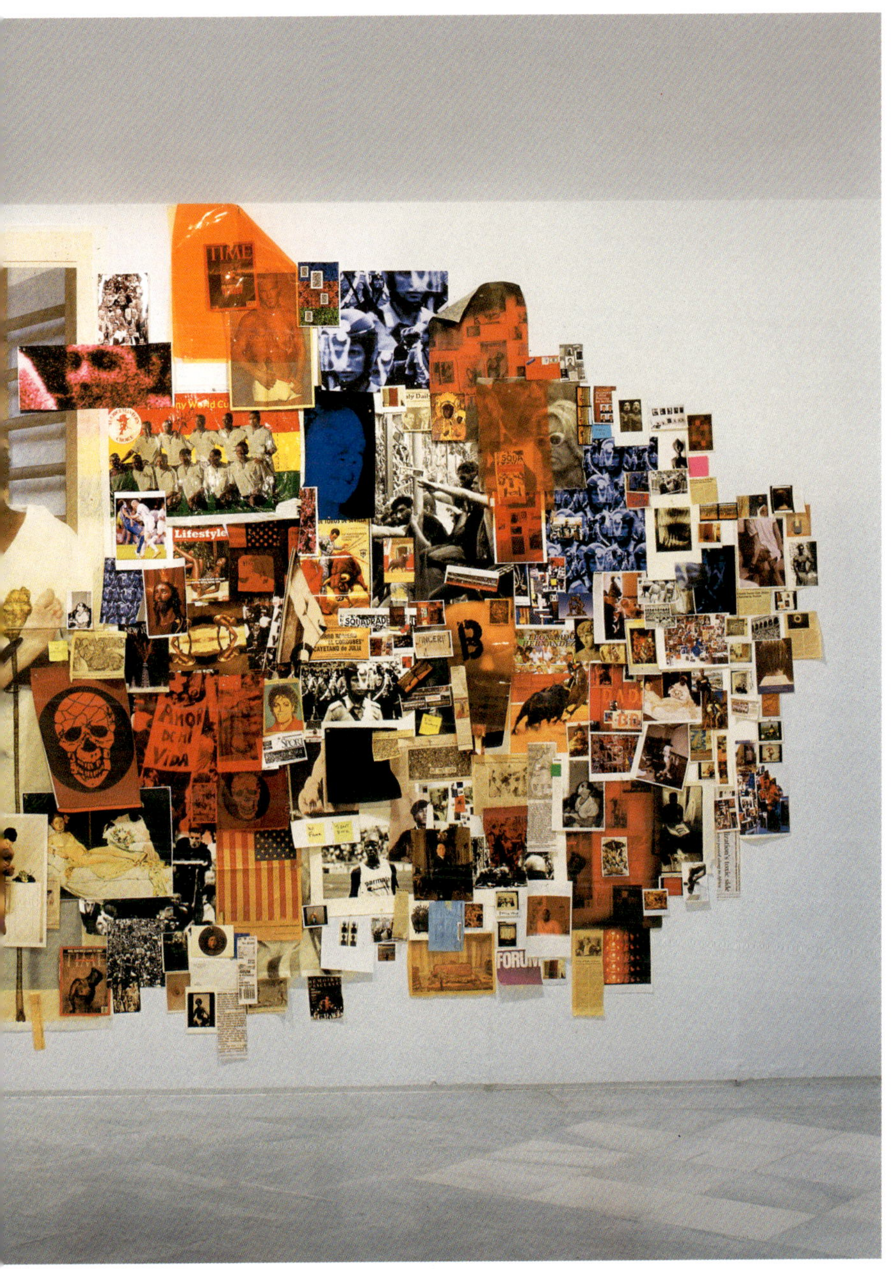

 Blow Up IV (Sevilla) 2006

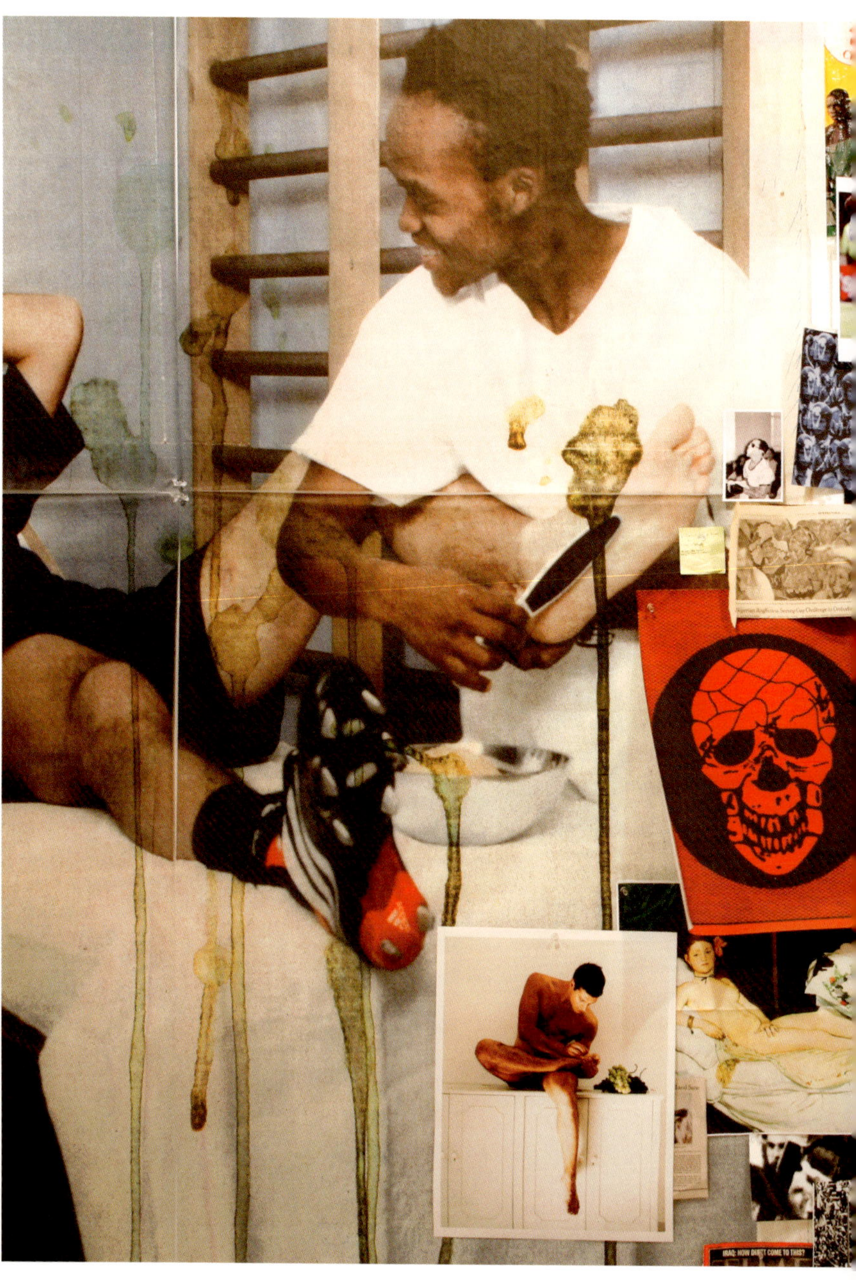
IRAQ: HOW DID IT COME TO THIS?

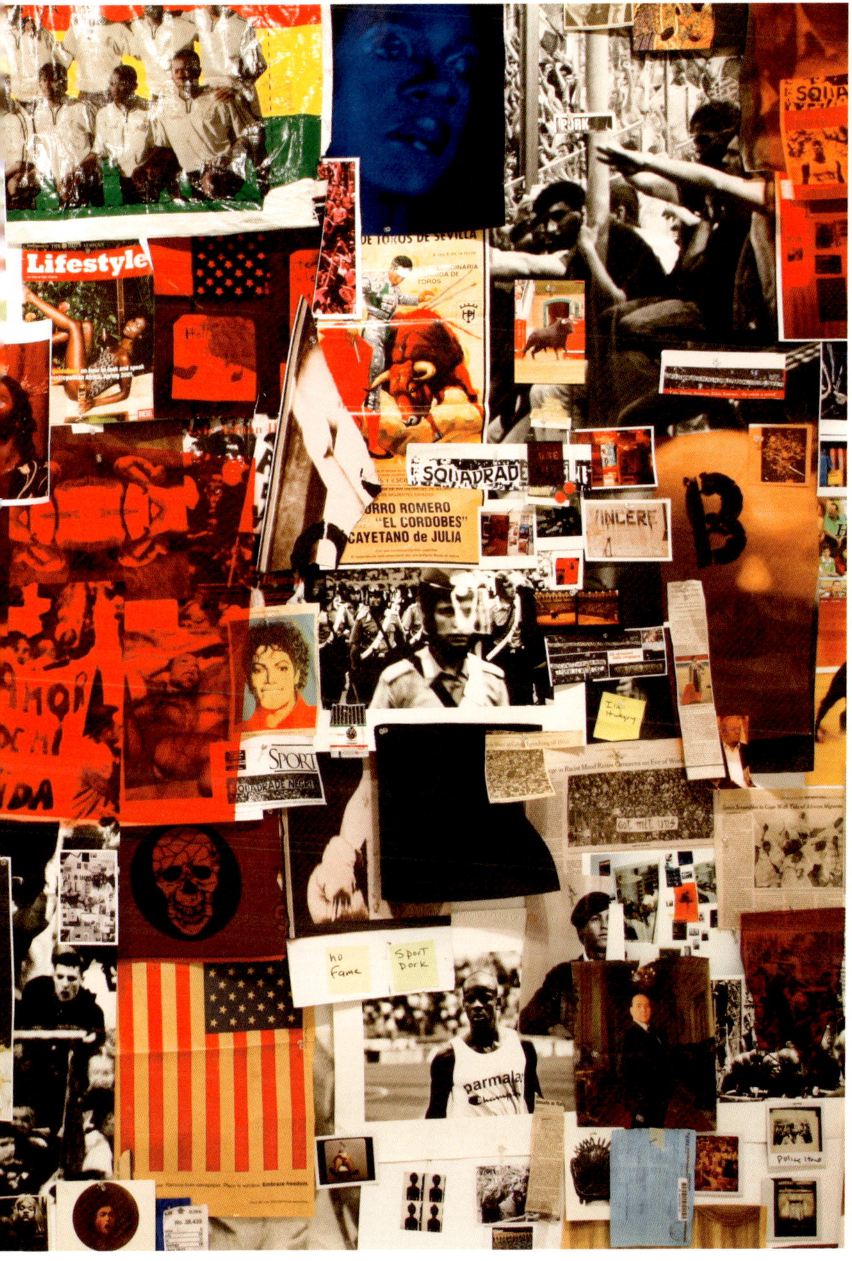

 Blow Up IV (Sevilla) 2006 (detail)

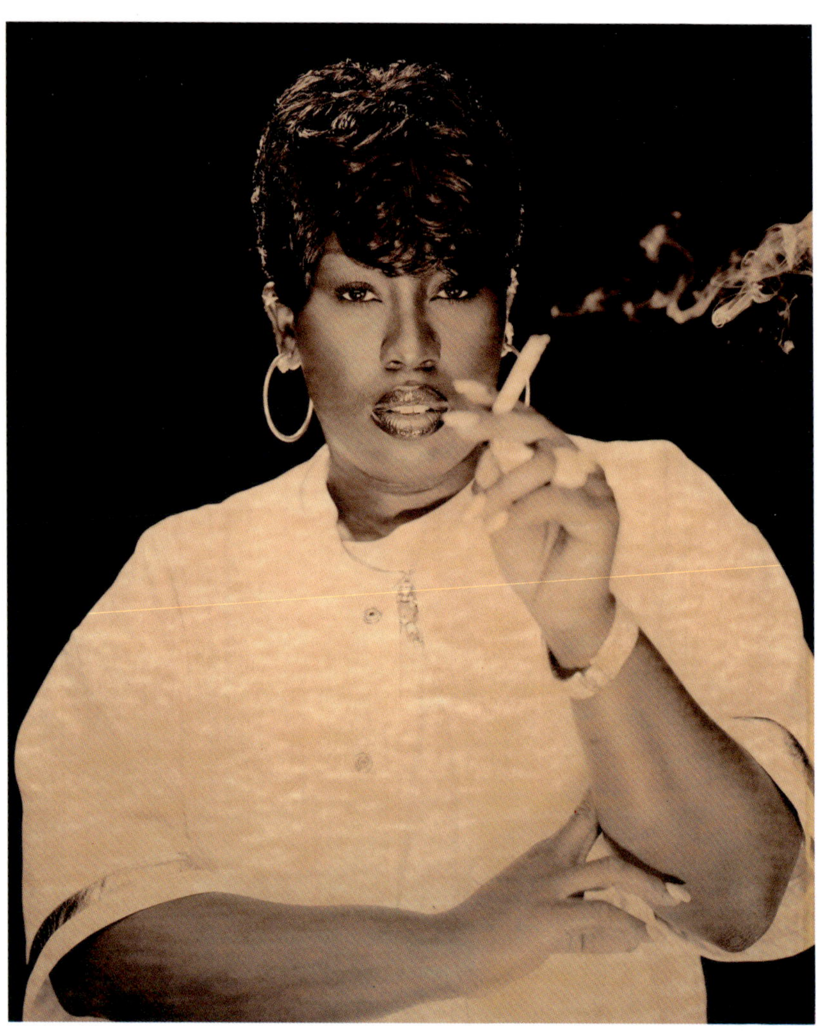

Untitled (*Missy Elliot #35*) 2000, published in *VIBE*, September 2000

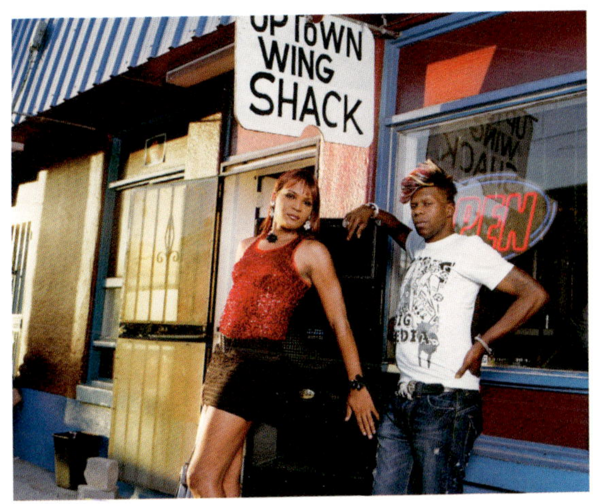

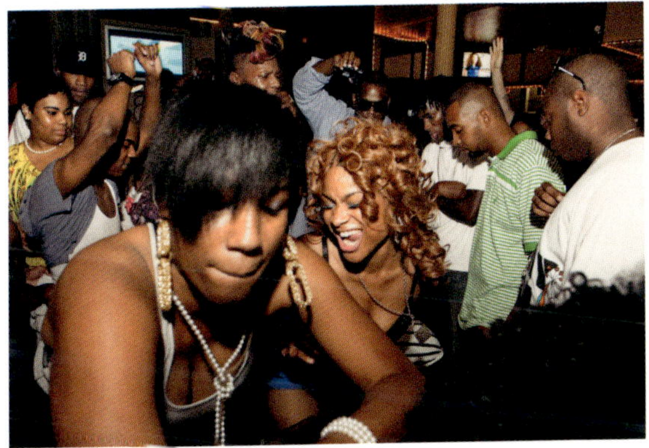

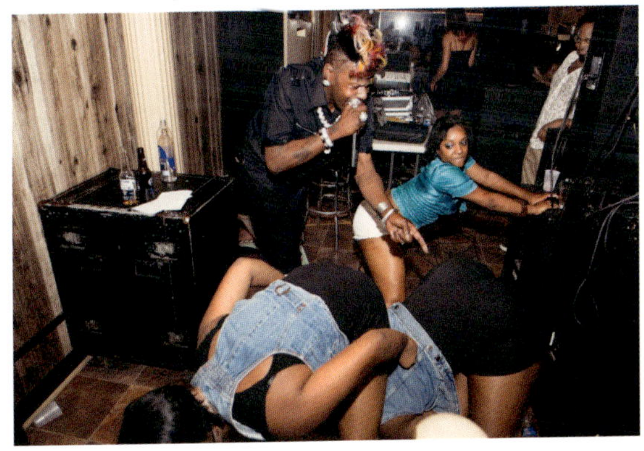

Top: Untitled (*Sissy Bounce #2*) 2011
Middle: Untitled (*Sissy Bounce #1*) 2011
Bottom: Untitled (*Sissy Bounce #3*) 2011
Published in *The New York Times Magazine*, 25 July 2010

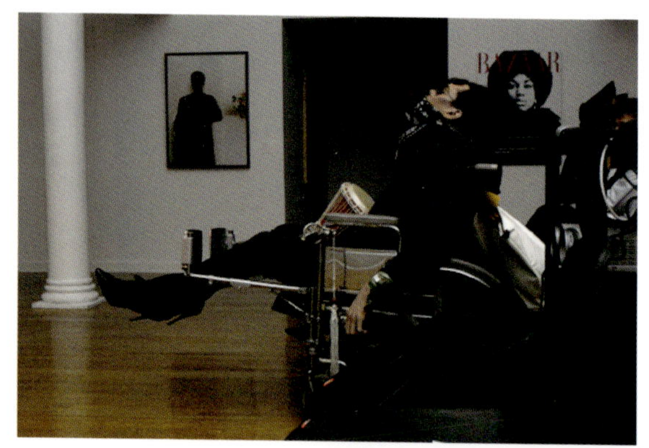

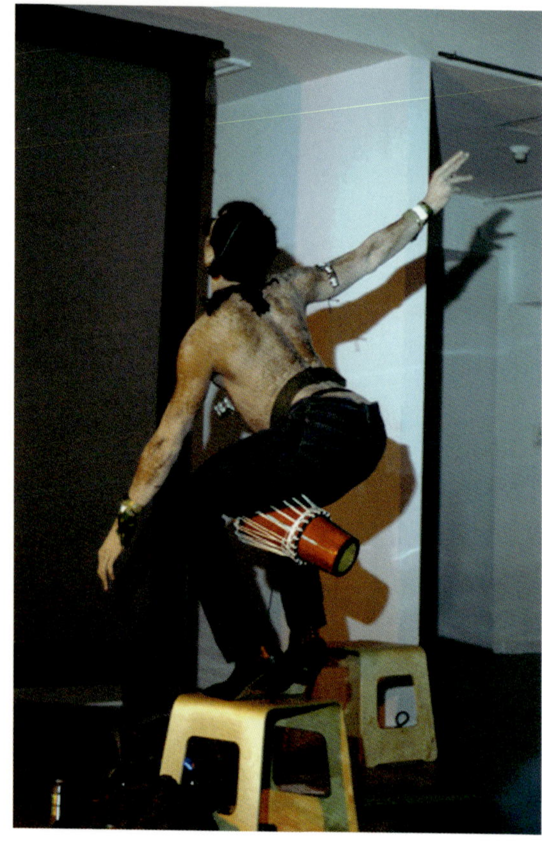

Above and opposite: *Performing MJ*, Vital Expressions in American Art Series, Studio Museum in Harlem, 2006. Photos: copyright Ray A. Llanos

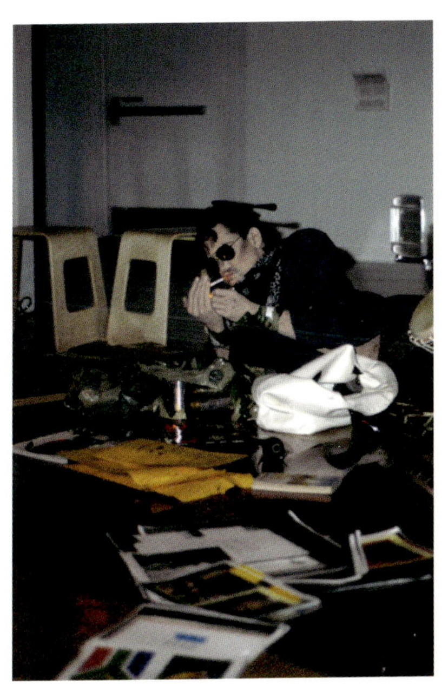

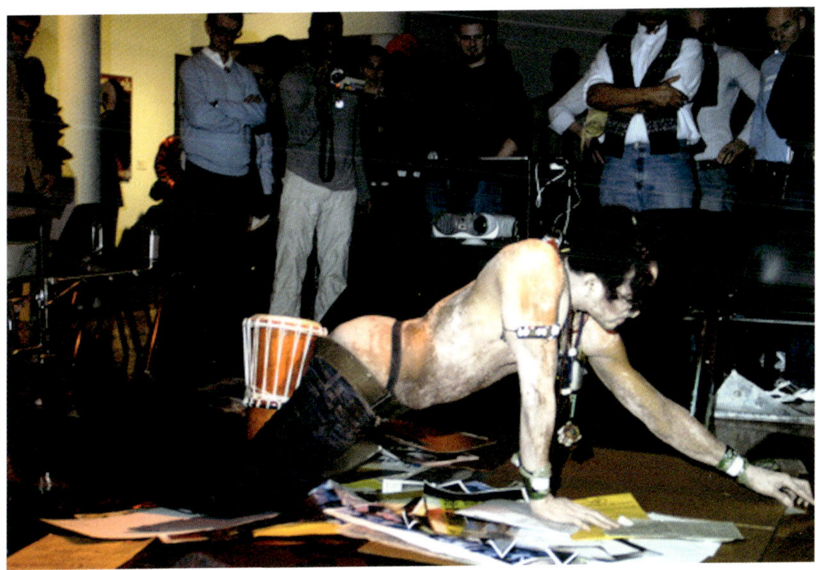

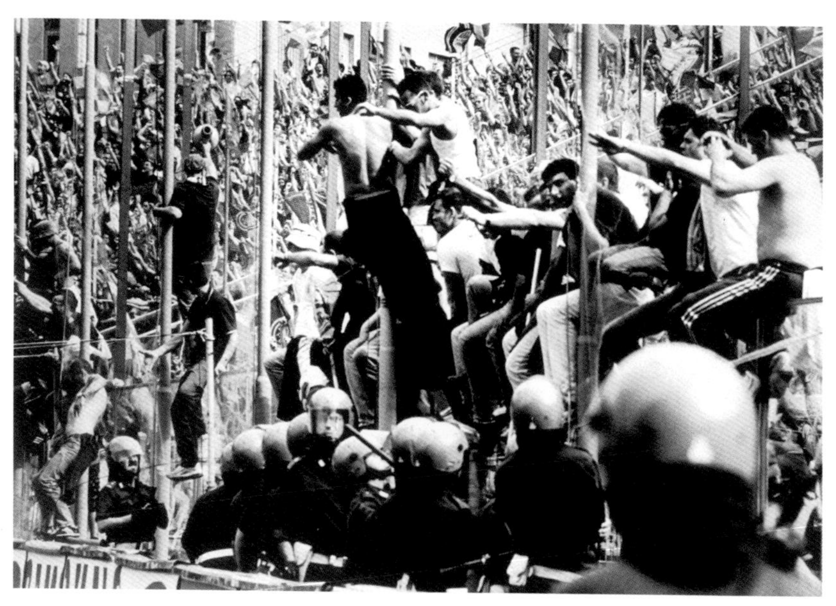

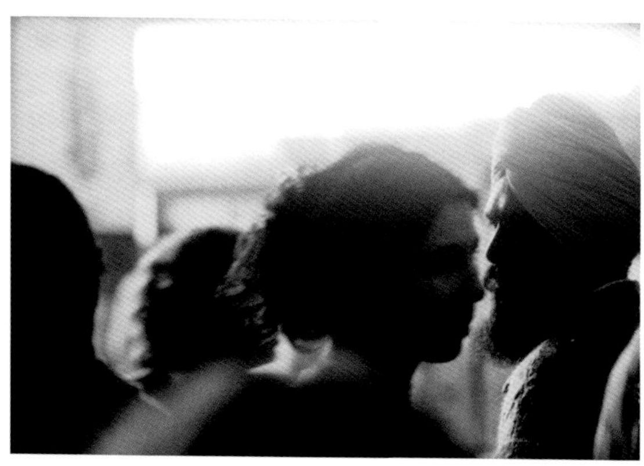

Top: *Verona #2* 2001 (Italia series)
Bottom: *Roman Stranger #7* 2001 (Italia series)

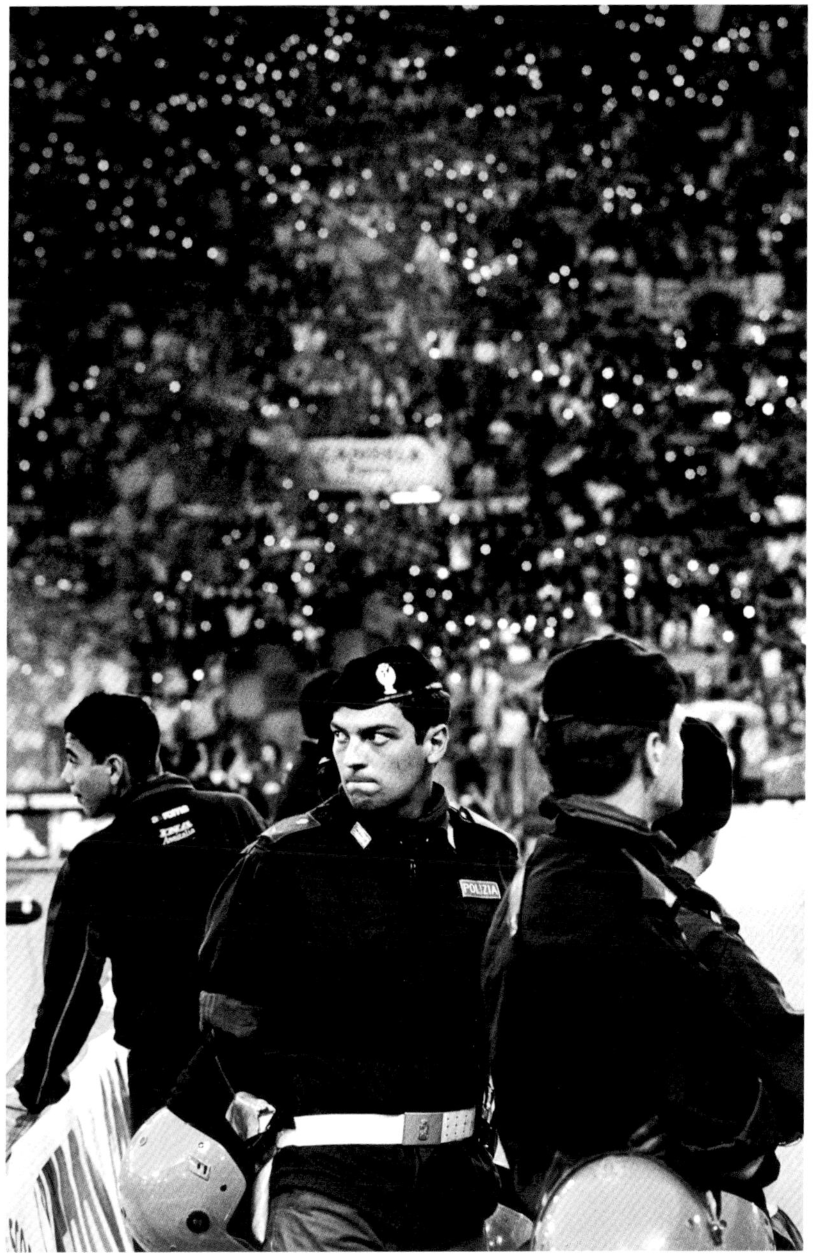

Polizia (Mille Luce) 2001 (Italia series)

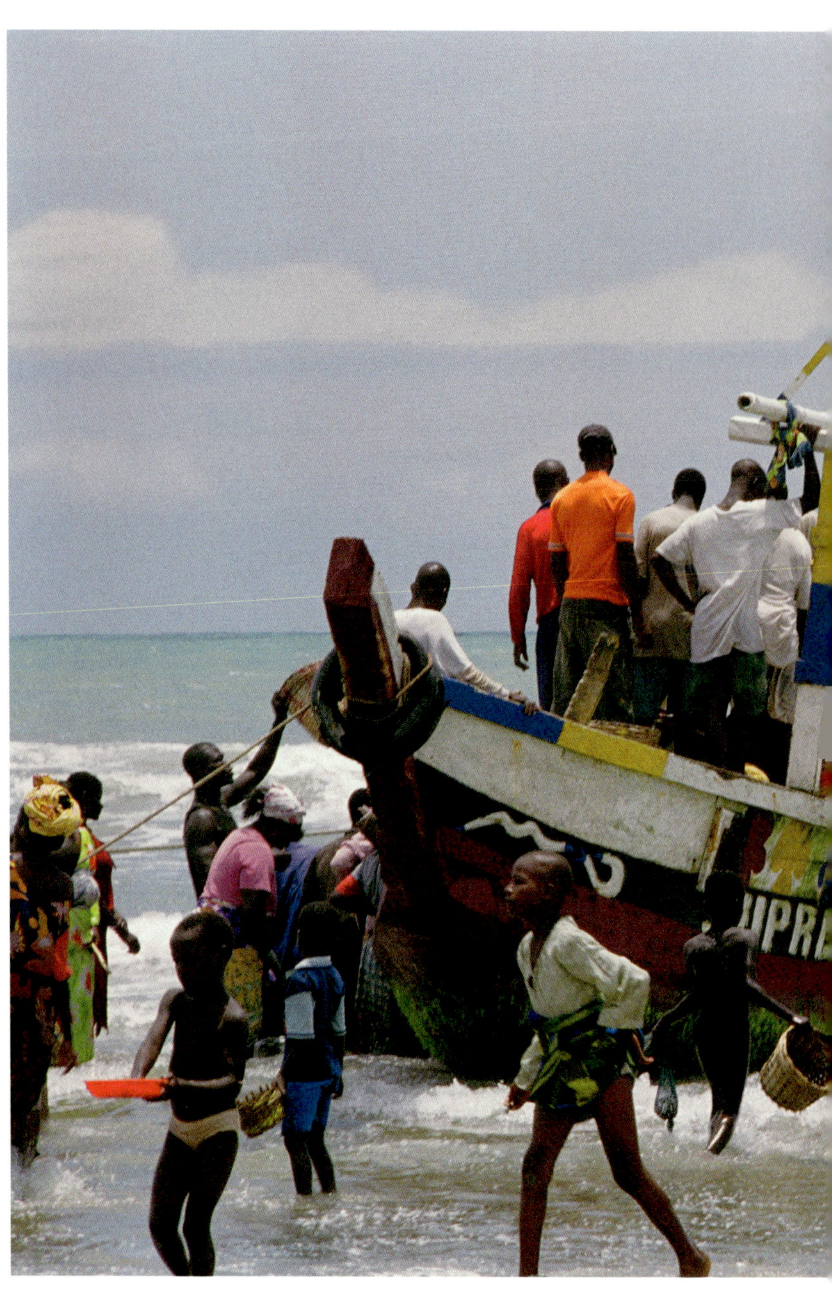

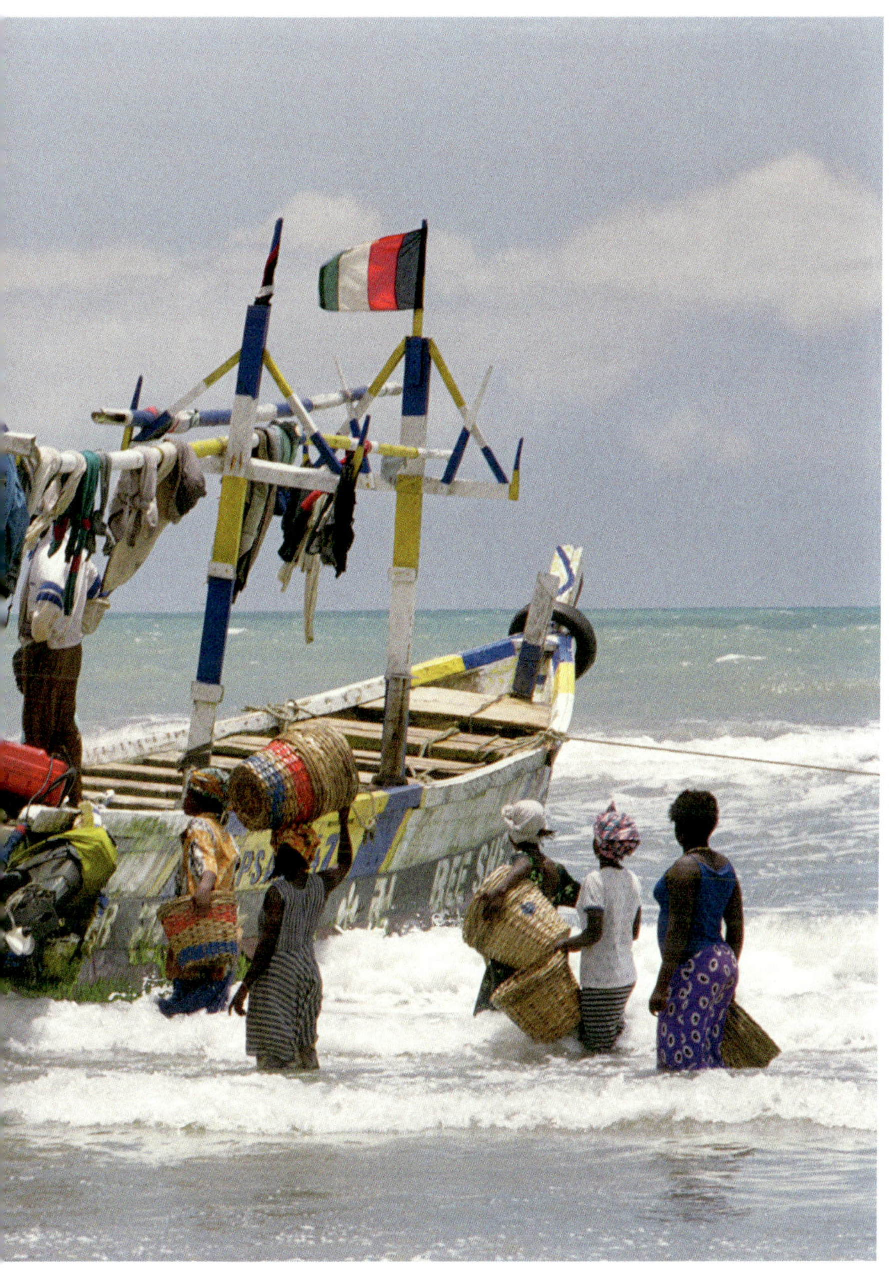

Untitled (*Kokrobitey #3*) 2008 (Ghana series)

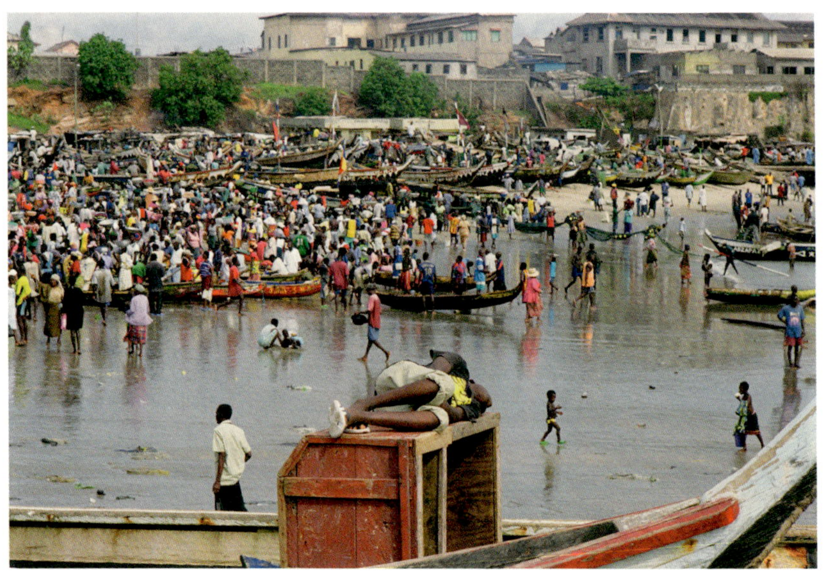

Untitled (*Jamestown* #6) 2008 (Ghana series)

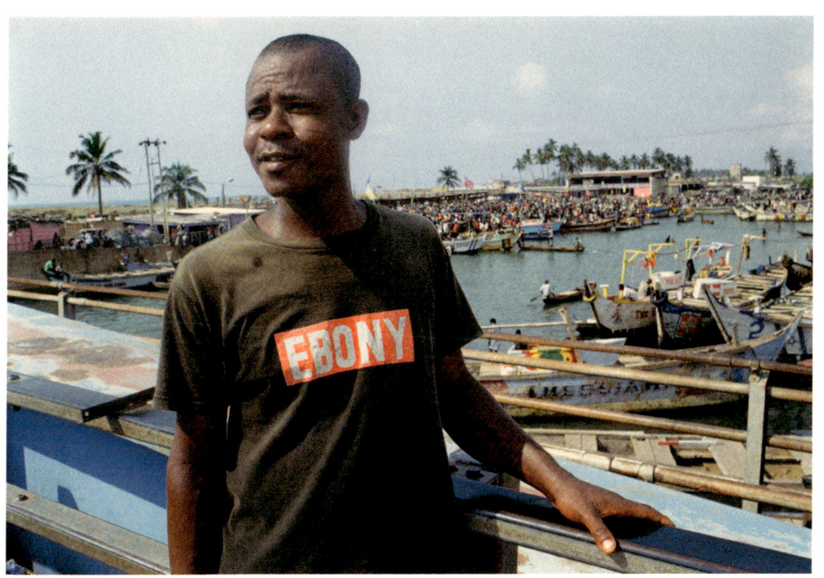

Untitled (*Elmina #1*) 2008 (Ghana series)

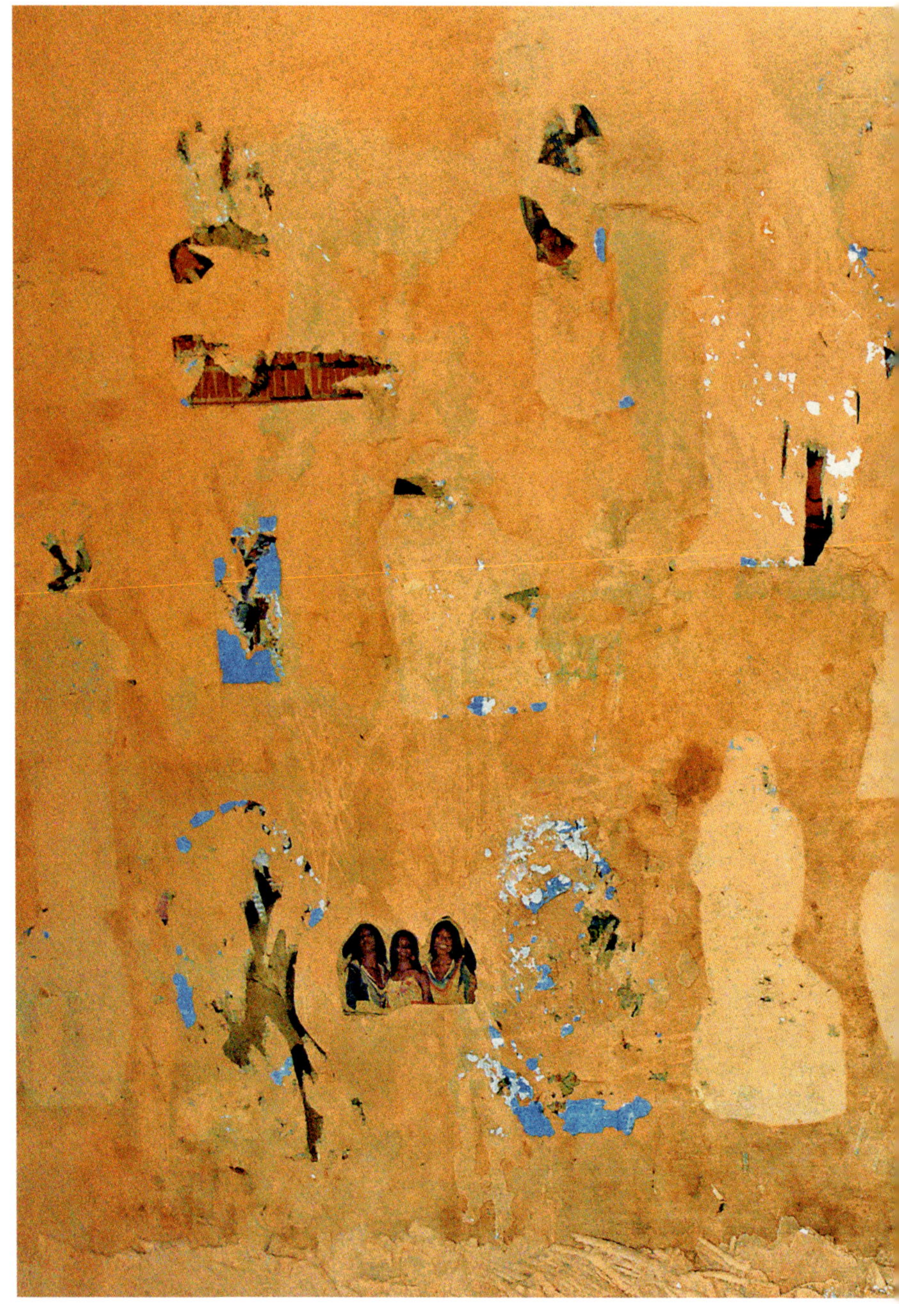

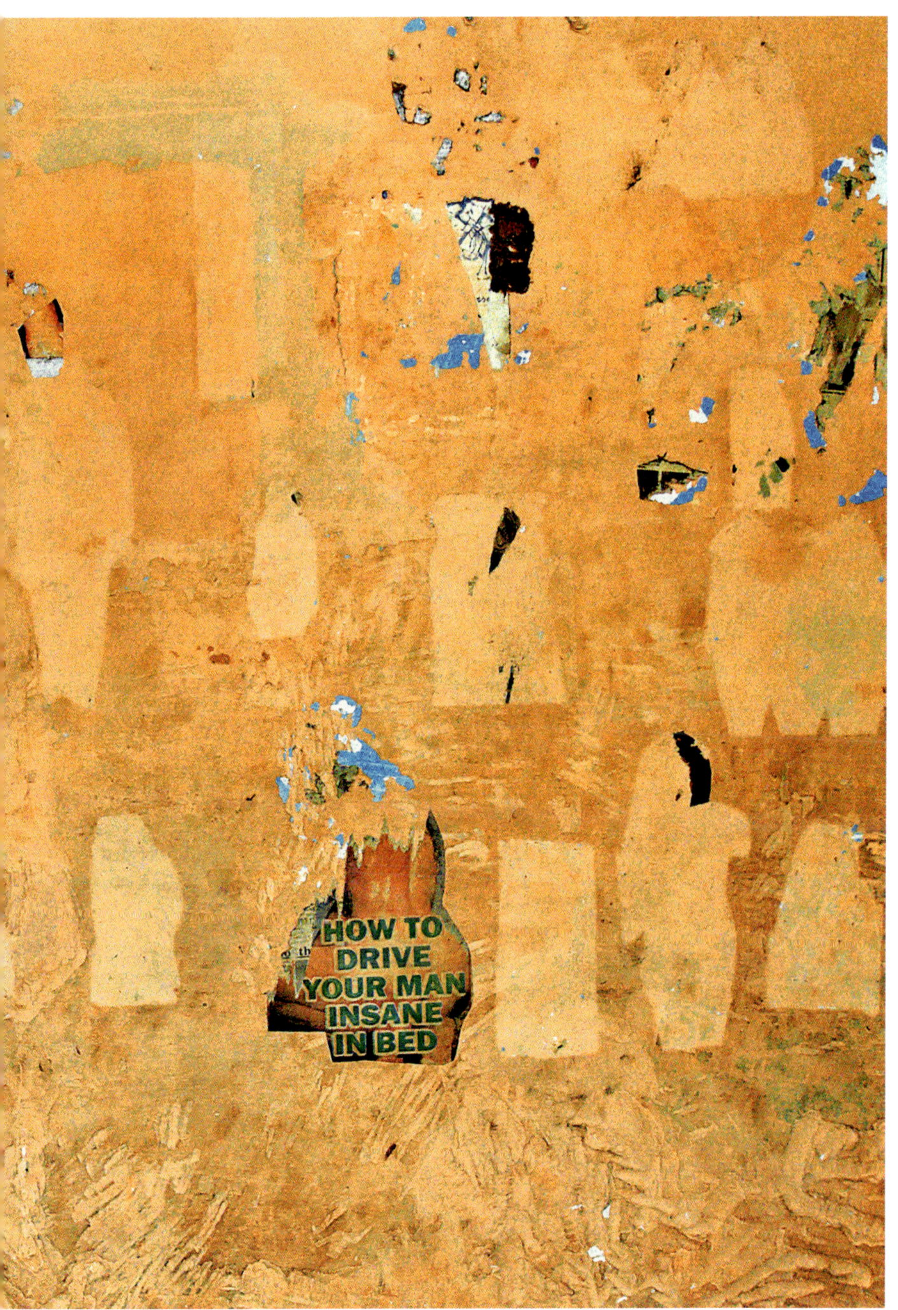

Untitled (*Erasure*) 2010 (Ghana series)

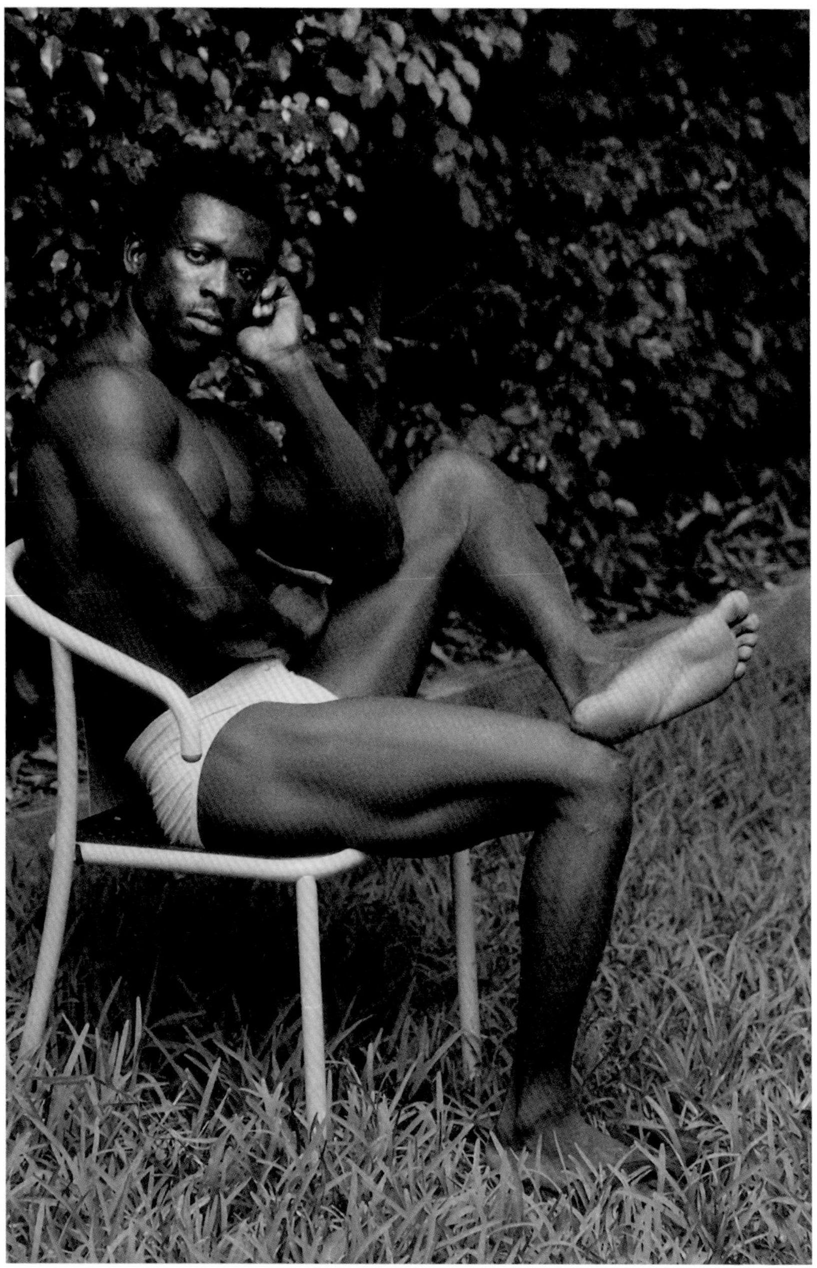

Untitled (*Prince, Accra, 2007*) 2023

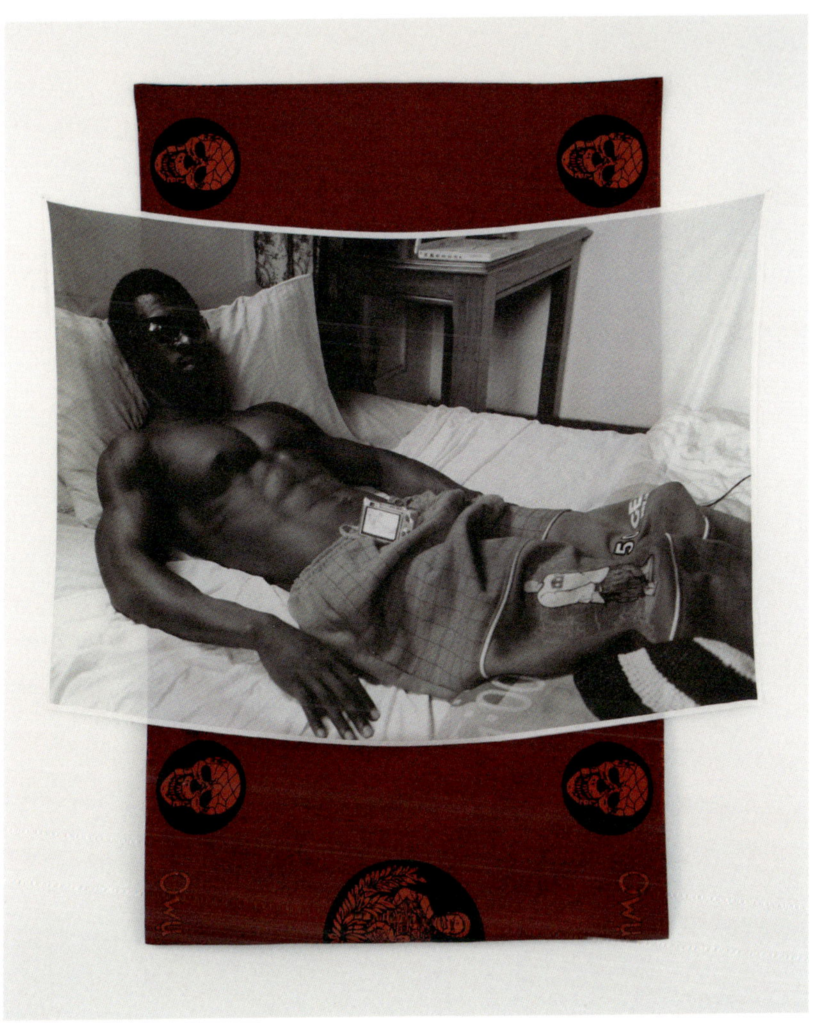

 Prince with Red Skulls 2013

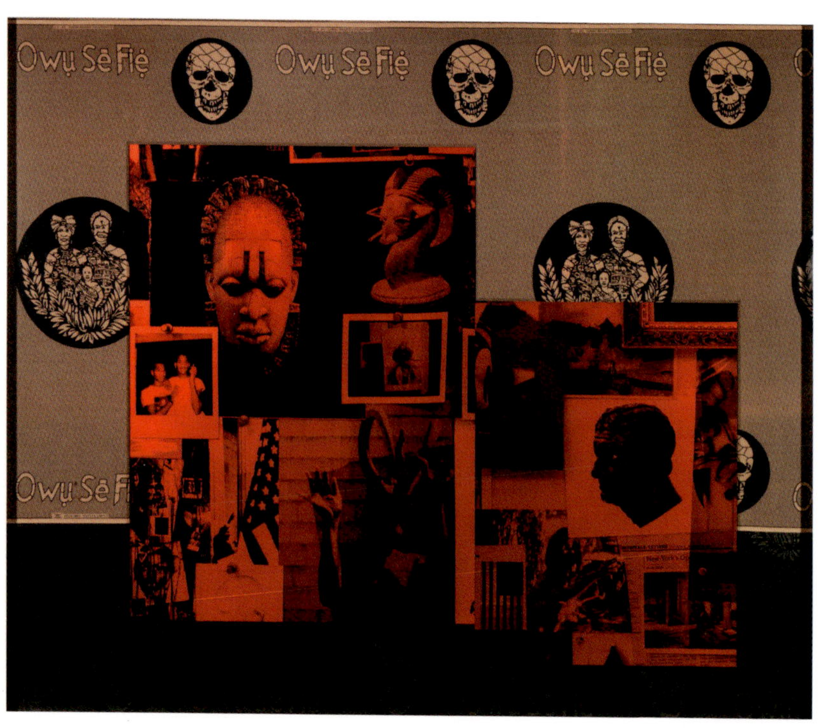

Ombre à l'Ombre 2019 (Shadow Works series)

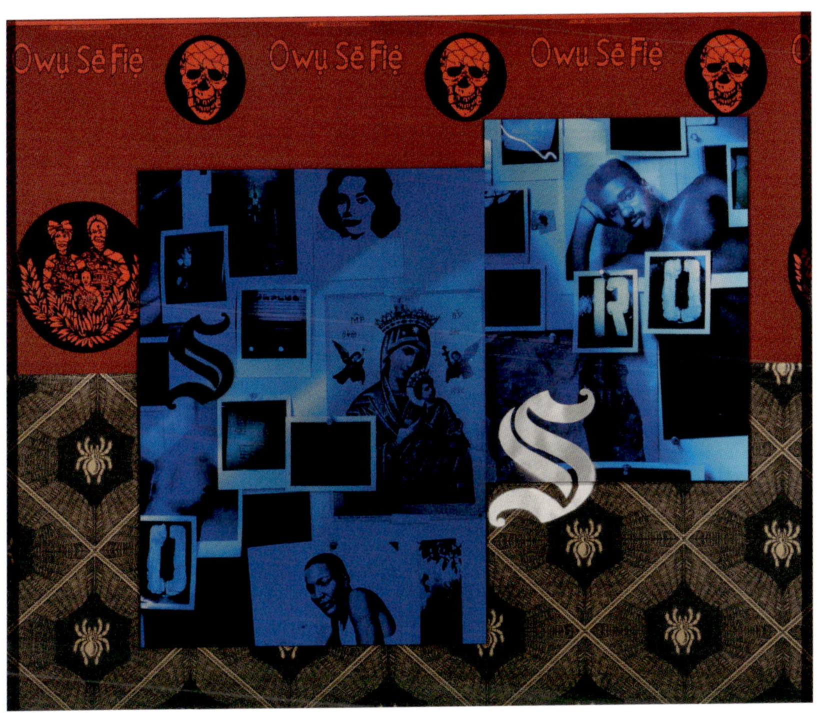

Anansi 2019 (Shadow Works series)

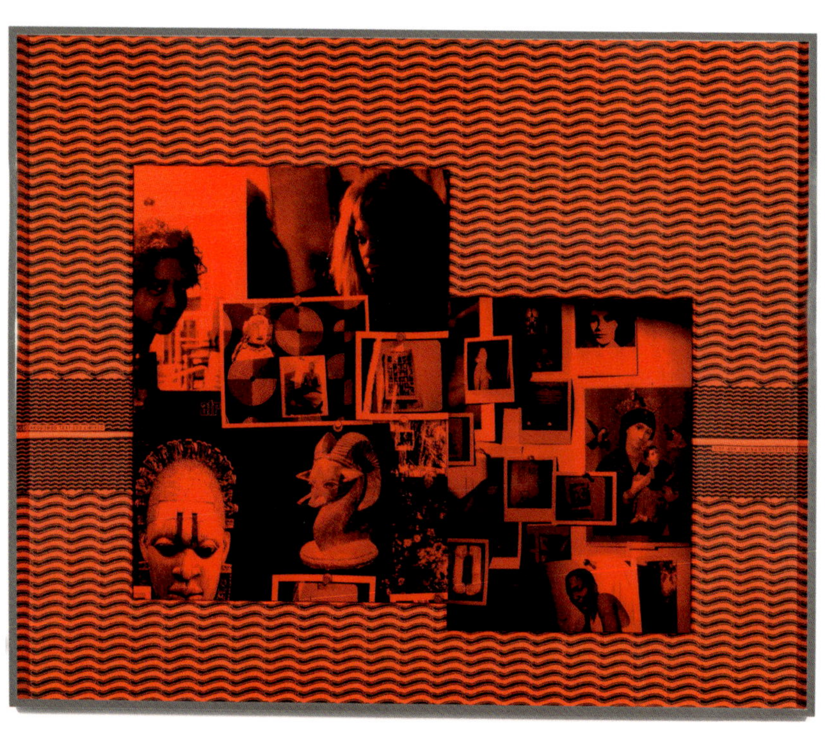

Above: *Queen Mother* 2019 (Shadow Works series)
Opposite: *Oracle* 2020 (Shadow Works series)

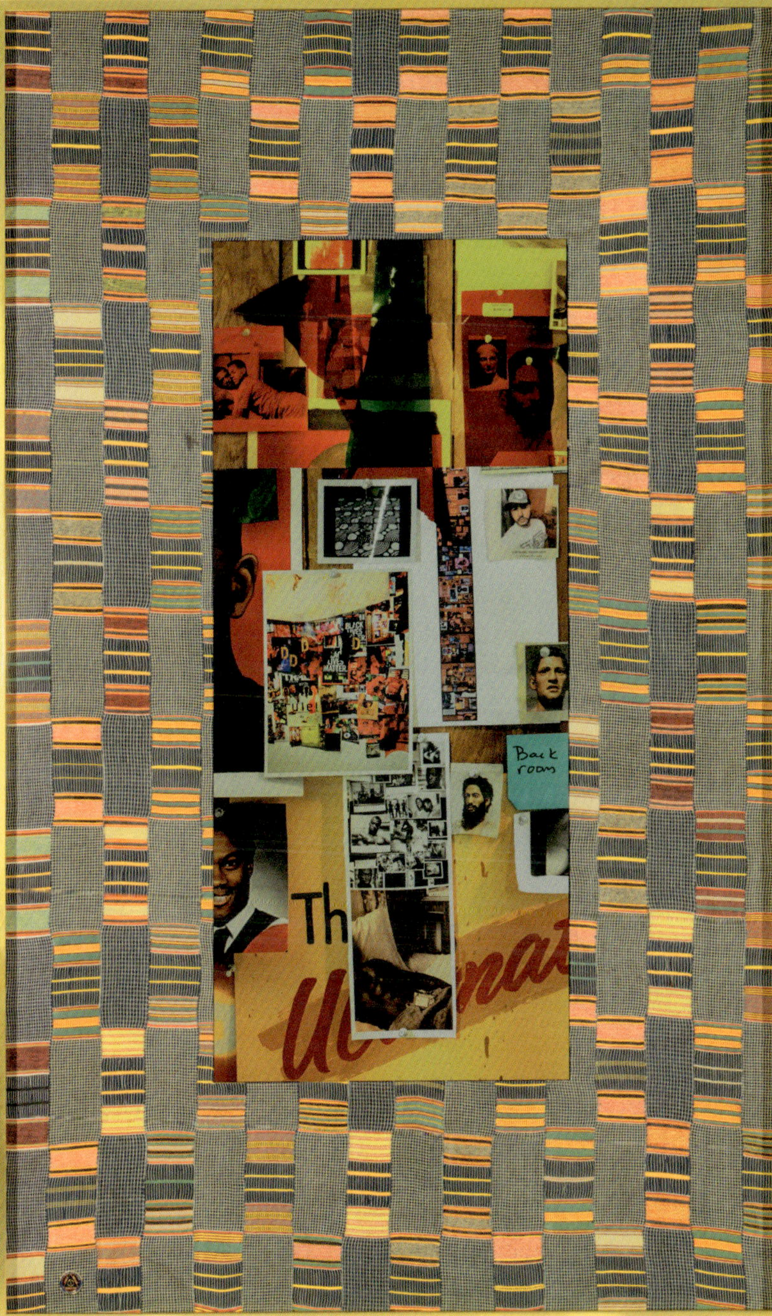
Back room
Th

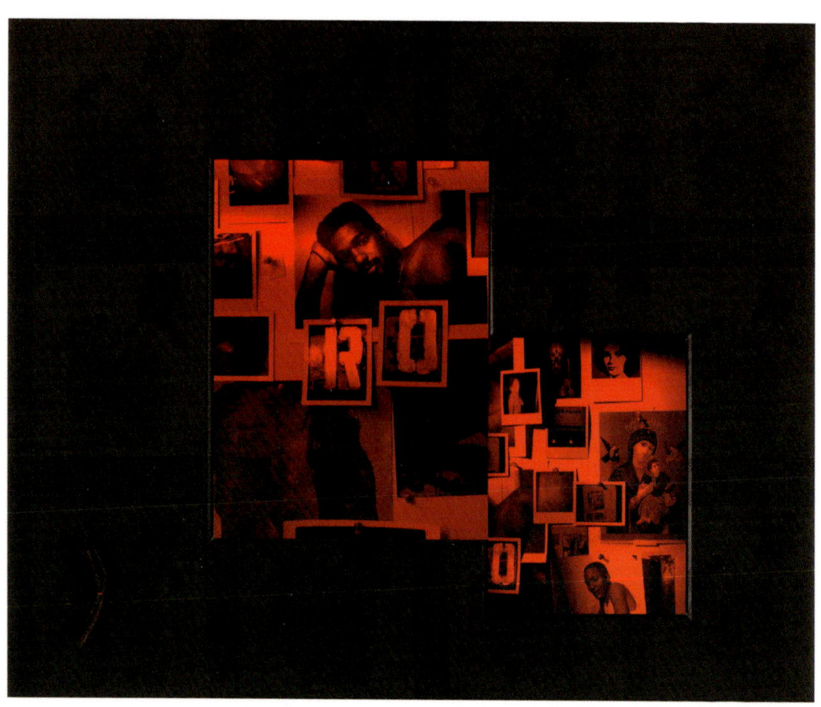

Untitled (*Black Hummingbird #1*) 2019 (Shadow Works series)

NOTES pp.8–16

1. bell hooks, *Talking Back: Thinking Feminist, Thinking Black*, 2nd edn, London 2014.
2. Okwui Enwezor, 'Excessive Exposure: The Polaroid Portraits of Lyle Ashton Harris', in Okwui Enwezor, *Lyle Ashton Harris: Excessive Exposure*, New York 2010, pp.1–34.
3. The first public exhibition curated by Autograph, which was established in 1988, titled *Autoportraits,* was presented at Camerawork in Bethnal Green, London, from 20 March – 12 April 1990 and featured works by Monika Baker, Allan DeSouza, Sunil Gupta, Lyle Ashton Harris, Mumtaz Karimjee and Roshini Kempadoo.
4. Conference titled *Regarding Michael Jackson: Performing Racial, Gender, and Sexual Difference Center Stage* presented at Yale University, 23–4 September 2004. Harris was invited by Hazel Carby, with whom he had studied while an undergraduate at Wesleyan University.
5. Lyle Ashton Harris and Anna Deavere Smith, *Lyle Ashton Harris*, New York 2004.

CREDITS

EDITOR'S ACKNOWLEDGEMENTS

Many thanks to Lyle Ashton Harris for being such a generous and inspiring collaborator on this book. Thanks to Yasufumi Nakamori for the invitation, and to Nicola Bion, Roz Hill and Bill Jones at Tate Publishing, and the designer Sarah Boris, for bringing it all together so effortlessly.

ARTIST'S ACKNOWLEDGEMENTS

I wish to express my sincere gratitude to all those who've contributed over the years to the legacy of *Constructs #10 – #13* 1989, and in particular for the work's acquisition by the Tate Americas Foundation through the support of its trustees and Agnes Gund, which prompted the publication of this volume in the Tate Photography Series.

I am especially thankful to Yasufumi Nakamori, who has been a staunch champion of my work at Tate, while leading the development of its photography collection in his former capacity as Senior Curator of International Art, Photography; to Mark Godfrey, former Tate Senior Curator, International Art, for guiding the museum to consider my early work for acquisition; and to Gregor Muir, Tate's Director of Collection, International Art, for welcoming my work into the museum's consummate collection. I am very appreciative of Tate Modern's Fiontán Moran, whose insightful engagement with my artworks and dexterous curatorial ingenuity bring fresh perspectives to the rich complexities of gender fluidity that widely resonate with the sensibilities of contemporary viewers.

I also wish to acknowledge the late photographer and theorist Allen Sekula, whose mentorship during his graduate photographic seminar at CalArts inspired an initial prototype of *Constructs*, as well as Monika Baker, Sunil Gupta and Autograph who organised a group exhibition in 1990 titled *Autoportraits* at Camerawork in London, which occasioned the first public presentation of *Constructs #10 – #13*. And the brilliant Thelma Golden is deserving of special mention for her inclusion of this work in her landmark exhibition *Black Male: Representations of Masculinity in Contemporary American Art* presented in 1994–5 at the Whitney Museum of American Art in New York City and the Hammer Museum in Los Angeles.

I continue to be thankful for the collaborative efforts among my current studio team – Ryan Rusiecki, Benjamin Hsu and Melia Chendo – whose ongoing oversight of production and operations greatly contributed to the realisation of this publication. And for his ceaseless dedication to my work since early in my career, my heartfelt thanks go to my dear friend Tommy Gear for his invaluable support and continuing presence in my life.